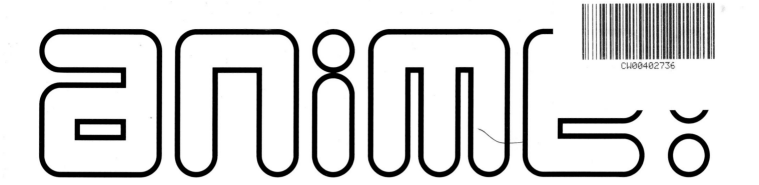

ANIME — a beginner's guide to the world of Japanese animation
ISBN 1 85286 492 3

Published by
Titan Books Ltd
19 Valentine Place
London SE1 8QH

Designer: Nigel Davies
Managing Editor: Katy Wild
Editor: David Barraclough
Production: Bob Kelly

First Titan edition October 1993
10 9 8 7 6 5 4 3 2 1

British Library Cataloguing-in-Publication Data. A catalogue record for this book is available from the British Library.

Printed and bound by Stephens and George Ltd, Merthyr Industrial Estate, Dowlais, Merthyr Tydfil.

Acknowledgements:

I would not even have considered writing this book had I not had before me the useful, informative and meticulously researched works of Frederick Schodt, the Kappa Boys (and girls!) of *Kappa Magazine*, and the various Granata Press publications. These didn't just supply information — they supplied inspiration. Many others have kindly provided me with information, pictorial material, assistance or encouragement, without which this book could not have been completed, and I extend my sincere thanks to them all. Special mention, however, must be given to a few individuals whose help has been especially valuable.

In Japan:
Ms Yukari Takeuchi of Tokyo Movie Shinsha Co Ltd
Ms Hiroko Akatsu of Bandai Visual Media Ltd

In the USA:
Ms Janice Hindle of AnimEigo

In Britain:
Nigel Fisher of Anime Projects
The staff and writers of *Anime UK Magazine*
Photographer extraordinare Sue Shadbolt
And, above all, my partner Steve Kyte

Photo Credits:

All pictures from the following productions are copyright as indicated and appear by the kind permission of Tokyo Movie Shinsha Co Ltd: *Aim for the Ace!* © Yamamoto S/TMS; *Cat's Eye* © Hojo T/Shueisha/TMS; *The Champion* © Takamori A/Tetsuya C/TMS; *Cobra* and *Space Adventure Cobra* © Teresawa B/TMS; *Georgie* © Igarashi Y/Izawa M/TMS; *God Mazinger* © Nagai G/Dynamic Planning/TMS; *God Mars* © Hikaru Prod/TMS; *Golgo 13* © Saitoh T/Saitoh Prod/TMS; *Hello Spank!* © Yukimuro S/Takanashi S/TMS; *Lupin III* © Monkey Punch/TMS/NTV/Toho; *Gigantor* © Hikari Prod/TMS; *Tetsujin 28-GO FX* © Hikari Prod/TMS/NAS/NTV; *Mon Pe* © Asatsu/TMS; *My Patraasche* © NTV/TMS; *Orguss* © Big West/TMS; *Rose of Versailles* © Ikeda R/TMS; *Space Fantasia R2001* © Hoshino Y/Takanashi S/TMS; *The Rescue Kids* © Monkey Punch/Sotsu Agcy/TMS; *Twins at St Clare's* © Darrel Waters Ltd/NTV/TMS.

All pictures from the following productions are copyright as indicated and appear by permission of the copyright holders with the kind assistance of AnimEigo: *Bubblegum Crisis* © AIC/Artmic/Network; *Bubblegum Crash* © AIC/Youmex; *Riding Bean* © Youmex; *Genesis Survivor Gaiarth* © Toshiba EMI; *Scramble Wars* © Artmic; *Gall Force* © Artmic.

All pictures from *Urusei Yatsura* are copyright Takahashi/Kitty Films and appear by permission of the copyright holders with the kind assistance of AnimEigo and Compass.

All pictures from the following productions are copyright as indicated and appear by permission of Bandai Visual Co Ltd with the kind assistance of Ms Hiroko Akatsu: *Dirty Pair: Project Eden* © Takachiho/Sunrise/NTV; *Dirty Pair: Flight 005 Conspiracy* © Takachiho/Sunrise.

All pictures from *The Sensualist* are copyright OB Planning Co/Studio JAMP Co and appear by permission of Western Connection with the kind assistance of Sasha Ciphkalo.

All pictures from the following productions are copyright as indicated and appear by permission of the copyright holders with the kind assistance of Kodansha and Manga Entertainment Limited: *Akira* © Akira Committee.

All pictures from *Astro Boy* are copyright Tezuka Productions and appear by permission of the copyright holders with the kind assistance of Mr Yoshihiro Shimizu.

All pictures from the following productions are copyright Dynamic Planning Co and appear by permission of Nagai Go with the kind assistance of Federico Colpi: *Devilman*.

All pictures from the following publications are copyright Dynamic Production Co Ltd and appear by permission of Nagai Go with the kind assistance of Federico Colpi: *Devilman*.

All pictures of phonecards appear by kind permission of Paul Bush.

All pictures of kits appear by kind permission of Paul Watson.

All photographs in this book, except that of Nagai Go on page 16, were taken by and are used by kind permission of Sue Shadbolt.

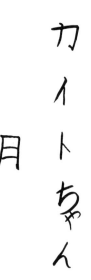

カイトちゃん
月

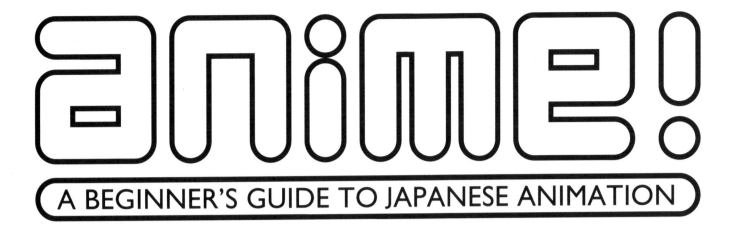

anime!

A BEGINNER'S GUIDE TO JAPANESE ANIMATION

TITAN BOOKS
LONDON

HELEN McCARTHY

Dirty Pair: Project Eden.

contents

an anime lexicon

Here is a guide to a few of the special terms and transliterated Japanese words you may encounter in English language anime and manga publications.

A note on pronunciation: in general, Japanese vowels are pronounced as short, crisp sounds. If you say the following sentence crisply and clearly, it's a good guide to the right sounds:

Ah, we soon get old
a   i   u   e   o

There are no vocal accents, though some Westerners mistake the double vowel symbol — a horizontal line over a letter, thus: ō — for an accent. Double vowels can also be written with a double letter (eg Ootomo for Otomo), but this misleads non-Japanese speakers into pronouncing the double o as in hoover. It should be pronounced exactly as the single vowel, but held for twice as long. Vowels appearing at the end of a Japanese word are audible. The acute French accent, sometimes employed by Western writers to indicate that the final 'e' of Anime is clearly pronounced, is not used in romanised Japanese.

A final note: throughout the book I have adopted the Japanese convention of family name first and personal name or initials last when mentioning Japanese names.

ANIME

The loanword for animation, borrowed by Japan from the Western word and now used by Western fans to distinguish the Japanese version from that of any other nation.

ANIPARO

ANIme PAROdy, a popular manga genre in which anime charas and situations are used in comic stories or skits.

BGM

BackGround Music — the music from an anime production.

BISHOJO/BISHONEN

Japanese word for beautiful young girl/boy, also generic terms for manga genre in which characters are drawn in a very stylised and ethereal fashion, with huge eyes.

-CHAN

Suffix meaning darling or little one, a term of affection usually reserved for small animals and children, romantic partners or young female friends. Used in anime in the eighties to describe 'squashed' versions of charas with enlarged heads and infant-style bodies.

CHARA

Loanword for CHARActer.

CB

From Child Body, the term now most often used for -chan versions of popular charas. Generally used as a prefix (eg CB Devilman).

GAIKOKUJIN

Japanese for foreigner. The term most usually heard, 'gaijin', actually means 'strange person', but was widely popularised in the West by William Gibson and other cyberpunk authors.

GARAGE KIT

A kit produced by a fan or fans working from home (originally in a garage or shed, hence the name) in small quantities and very basic packaging. Garage kits have now become a major industry in their own right, with some of the original garage kit producers becoming large companies, and new ones springing up all the time. Usually more complex, more accurate, or based on rarer charas and mecha than mainstream, mass produced kits.

GEKIGA

Japanese term for graphic novel.

IDOL SINGER

Japanese term for a particular type of chara — usually young, cute and female — and her voice artist. Both generally enjoy short but hectic pop music careers that last as long as their cute looks.

IMAGE ALBUM

Music inspired by or based on, but not taken directly from, the soundtrack of an anime film.

JAPLISH

Word used to refer to the uncanny Japanese ability to write English with an offbeat view of the structure of the language! To achieve Japlish perfection, a phrase or sentence should make its meaning obvious in context but be incomprehensible on a purely literal level (eg Attacked Mystification Police Department).

KAMI

Japanese word for god or goddess, applied as a term of the greatest respect, eg the great manga artist and animator Tezuka, often referred to as 'manga no kami' (the manga god); or, with the suffix -sama (a very rarely used form) as a superlative description, eg 'kawaii no kamisama' (the Great God/dess of Cute).

KAWAII

Japanese for cute. Cuteness is a characteristic of national importance in Japan and many anime charas are cute in the extreme.

LOANWORD

A word borrowed from another language (usually Western) and incorporated into Japanese (eg anime).

MANGA

Japanese for comic. The term was coined in 1815 by the great artist Hokusai and is usually translated as 'irresponsible pictures'. It stuck to the products of the comic industry. Never used in Japan for moving pictures, although in the UK the Manga Video label uses the term 'manga movies' extensively to describe anime released on their own label.

MECHA

Loanword for MECHAnical, meaning any kind of machinery, from a simple gun to a combat tank or giant robot.

MOBILE SUIT

Acronym coined by Tomino Yoshiyuki to describe the giant humanoid fighting machines in his epic series *Mobile Suit Gundam*. These require one or more human operators inside them to function. Many so-called 'giant robots' are in fact mobile suits — the true robot can function through a remote control unit or via an internal system without the need for an onboard human operator. Sometimes abbreviated to MS.

NEWTYPE

Term coined by Tomino for *MS Gundam* to describe a spontaneous genetic mutation within the human organism, usually occurring among those with either a talent for or a connection with work in space; it can also be artificially produced, though artificial NewTypes tend to be dangerously unstable personalities. NewTypes have an affinity for technology, the most powerful being able to run huge and complex weapon systems purely by the power of thought. They are telepaths and often also empaths. NewTypes are found under that name only in the *Gundam* universe, but other manga and anime writers and directors have been influenced by the concept.

OAV

Original Animation Video (also referred to as OVA), a work made onto video rather than for TV or cinema. Because of the lower costs involved, many of the more eccentric or specialised new works are released as OAVs.

OST

Original Sound Track, ie the music of anime production, including all songs.

OTAKU

Japanese word meaning obsessive, in the sense of being narrow, selfish and not interested in social interaction. Anime fans are often described as 'otaku no video', generally translated as 'video fanboy'. It is a term of strong condemnation in Japan; however, some Western fans view the label as a medal of honour rather than a badge of shame. An otaku is someone with the flexibility and breadth of interest to step outside the pulp entertainments offered by their own culture and look beyond.

SD

From Super Deformed, usually used as a prefix (eg *SD Gundam*). A more manic and mischievous, less innocent version of the CB/-chan concept.

SENSEI

Japanese word meaning master or teacher; a term of respect applied only to the acknowledged giants in a field, as a suffix to the surname (eg Tezuka-sensei, Nagai-sensei). Also used alone as a form of address.

introduction

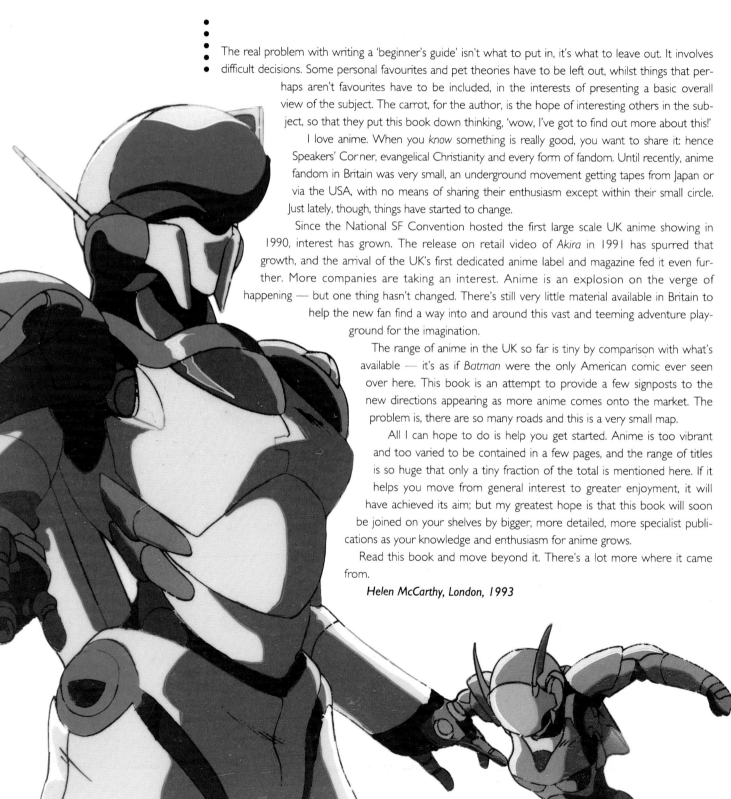

The real problem with writing a 'beginner's guide' isn't what to put in, it's what to leave out. It involves difficult decisions. Some personal favourites and pet theories have to be left out, whilst things that perhaps aren't favourites have to be included, in the interests of presenting a basic overall view of the subject. The carrot, for the author, is the hope of interesting others in the subject, so that they put this book down thinking, 'wow, I've got to find out more about this!'

I love anime. When you *know* something is really good, you want to share it: hence Speakers' Corner, evangelical Christianity and every form of fandom. Until recently, anime fandom in Britain was very small, an underground movement getting tapes from Japan or via the USA, with no means of sharing their enthusiasm except within their small circle. Just lately, though, things have started to change.

Since the National SF Convention hosted the first large scale UK anime showing in 1990, interest has grown. The release on retail video of *Akira* in 1991 has spurred that growth, and the arrival of the UK's first dedicated anime label and magazine fed it even further. More companies are taking an interest. Anime is an explosion on the verge of happening — but one thing hasn't changed. There's still very little material available in Britain to help the new fan find a way into and around this vast and teeming adventure playground for the imagination.

The range of anime in the UK so far is tiny by comparison with what's available — it's as if *Batman* were the only American comic ever seen over here. This book is an attempt to provide a few signposts to the new directions appearing as more anime comes onto the market. The problem is, there are so many roads and this is a very small map.

All I can hope to do is help you get started. Anime is too vibrant and too varied to be contained in a few pages, and the range of titles is so huge that only a tiny fraction of the total is mentioned here. If it helps you move from general interest to greater enjoyment, it will have achieved its aim; but my greatest hope is that this book will soon be joined on your shelves by bigger, more detailed, more specialist publications as your knowledge and enthusiasm for anime grows.

Read this book and move beyond it. There's a lot more where it came from.

Helen McCarthy, London, 1993

↱ *Original Hokusai manga, c. 1818 – an "irresponsible picture".*

from history to technology

1

THE EARLY YEARS OF ANIME

Iron Man flying into action in the 1980 TV series.

Otomo Katsuhiro's animated film *Akira* appeared at the Piccadilly Film Festival in the summer of 1990 and stunned London. In April 1991, following further screenings, Island World Communications (now Manga Entertainment Ltd) acquired the film for release in the UK on retail video. Its success led IWC to set up a UK retail label for Japanese animation — called Manga Video, to trade on the existing familiarity their target market, twelve to nineteen year-old British males, had with the Japanese word for comics — and ever since anime has grown in popularity. The medium is now poised for a major breakthrough into the mainstream of Western pop culture. It may come as a surprise, then, to learn that not only is it an old-established form with a long history in its own country, but that we in Europe have been in contact with anime from its beginnings in the early years of this century.

Japanese animation grew from the long tradition of popular narrative scroll paintings of the medieval period, via the popular woodblock print series of such masters as Hokusai and the widespread availability of books and periodicals in the nineteenth century. Manga — comic books and strips — was already well established by the early years of this century, when the newer art of film was becoming increasingly popular.

Early collaborations between Japanese artists and cartoonists produced animated work from so far removed from the traditions of Japanese folk art, with their sense of the ridiculous, their gross exaggeration of physical characteristics for dramatic or comic purpose, their anthropomorphic animals and clean, simple lines, and their influences were readily absorbed. Tezuka moved the manga strip away from the 'talking heads' style prevalent at the time and back to its roots, his expressive narrative drawings blending the styles of earlier Japanese art with the influences of the movies. He gave manga a new visual vocabulary, and took it with him into anime.

The young Tezuka decided to become a doctor, but nevertheless had no intention of giving up his early ambition to create manga and make his own animated films. In 1946, at the age of seventeen, he got his chance through a neighbour who worked on a children's publication. His regular strip, *Ma-Chan's Diary*,

Iron Man.

Gigantor — the robot and his young pilot Shotaro Kaneda.

around 1914, and anime headed West when Kitayama Seitaro's 1918 film, *Momotaro*, enjoyed success in Europe. The first Japanese anime talkie, *Chikara To Onna No Yononaka*, appeared in 1932, directed by Masaoka Kenzo, and the first full-length colour anime film of the modern era was Yabushita Taiji's *Hakujaden*, released by Toei Doga in 1958 and winner of a major award at the 1959 Venice Children's Film Festival. Influences from Western film affected the Japanese industry and anime was no exception; Disney, the Fleischer brothers and Europeans like Jiri Trnka and Walerian Borowczyk were all widely known.

It was before the Second World War that the man who gave the anime industry its impetus was first hooked by the charm of the cartoon. Tezuka Osamu came into contact with the works of Disney and the Fleischers through his high school film club. He was already a prolific cartoonist; some 3,000 pages of his earliest manga survived his school years during the Pacific bombings and give evidence of a precocious talent. The American animated films of the period were not

was a success and a year later his first solo manga made him an overnight sensation. He became the biggest selling manga artist in Japan while still studying at university for his medical degree.

His manga were so popular that Toei Doga, one of Japan's most respected film companies, approached him about making anime adaptations. In the early sixties he set up his own production company, Mushi Productions, with the first Mushi film, *The Story of a Certain Street Corner*

Early Japanese gekiga.

The FX support team — Kaneda,

Sakuro, Yoko and Futaba.

One of Iron Man's opponents.

Baddie-mech Tetsujin 28
Black DX.

(*Aru Machikado No Monogatari*) appearing in 1962. The honour of producing the first anime TV series does not, as is often assumed, belong to Tezuka and Mushi — *Astro Boy* (*Tetsuwan Atom*) started its TV run after the Otagi company's *Manga Calendar*, which ran from June 1962 to August 1964 — but Tezuka gave the fledgling anime industry an impetus which has scarcely flagged since. Inspired by the dynamic young artist and writer, a new generation of animators began producing entertainment for TV and cinema.

Tezuka's works, and those of his disciples, made use of both the romantic adventure story and the science fiction genre to explore the significance of Japan's defeat and near-destruction in World War Two, and to look for ways in which she could be reborn. Again and again, the

themes of Armageddon, of death and destruction, of rebirth through sacrifice and unselfishness, are played out by humans and animals, aliens and insects, in space, in the far past or future, in the jungle or the realms of fantasy. Familiar historical events and folktales were also used as the basis for allegorical stories of struggle, survival and rebirth.

The decade following Hiroshima saw Japan realising the need to modernise and expand into new industries for survival. Technology, regarded in Europe with deep suspicion ever since the Industrial Revolution, offered the Japanese the prospect of something much better than mere survival — success. Buying Western expertise where necessary, the Japanese would work hard and improve on it. The first nation to make extensive use of the industrial robot is still the world's largest user of robot technology, and Japanese popular entertainment mirrors the general enthusiasm for the concept of the 'tin man'.

Most often thought of in the West as close kin to Frankenstein's monster, the robot in Japan — especially in anime — is a friend, a helper and a way of giving the little man an even chance in a big and hostile world. Probably the closest Western parallel to the upbeat, infectious enthusiasm of the Japanese for technology is the technophilia found in the 1960s TV series of Gerry and Sylvia Anderson, creators of *Thunderbirds*. Here it is a great benefit to mankind and the dangers come only from human carelessness or misuse. Manga and anime have helped to encourage and maintain Japan's positive attitude to technology, and by making it both popular and acceptable have thus contributed considerably to the nation's progress and prosperity.

Technology's first non-human face in anime was not that of a fearsome, threatening creature cobbled together from the grave, but a cheerful little boy. In 1963, Tezuka created *Astro Boy*, Japan's second anime TV series, a reworking of the Pinocchio legend for the twenty-first century. A scientist whose son has been killed in a car crash creates a robot in his image. The little robot wants to become fully human, but meanwhile uses his strength and skills to help mankind. Based on Tezuka's hugely successful manga series *Ambassador Atom* (*Atom Taishi*), which ran from 1951 to 1968 in *Shonen Magazine*, the adventures of the Atom were presented in 1959 in a live-action TV series, but it was anime that realised their full potential. The series was soon sold to the USA for TV screening, and is still popular there, as shown by its recent release by US video company The Right Stuf, Inc.

Another great robot legend was born in 1963 and also gained popularity in the States — Iron Man No 28 (Tetsujin 28-GO) starred in the TV series of the same name from TCJ. Based on Yokoyama Mitsuteru's manga, the tale of the remote-controlled fighter for justice and peace differs from that of *Astro Boy* in one vital respect. The Atom is a robot capable of independent thought and action, and can choose between good and evil, but Iron Man is simply a machine, directed by whoever holds its control box at the time.

These two types of robot crop up again throughout the history of anime. The giant robot genre has enduring popularity, but still refers back, frequently and with renewed insight as well as affectionate respect, to the themes laid down by Tezuka and Yokoyama four decades ago: how the use of artificial means to enhance man's power can both help and deceive us, how humanity can have origins and foundations other than flesh, and how far man is responsible for the effects of his creations on the rest of the universe.

In fact, 1963 proved a seminal year, as it also saw the first appearance of the cyberman in anime. TCJ again took a fascinating concept, this time from Kuwata and Hirai's manga *Eight Man*, and televised it as a series. Murdered detective Azuma Hachiro had his mind and memories transferred to an android body a quarter of a century

before *RoboCop* hit the screens. *Eight Man* was also shown in the USA and is now enjoying a revival on video.

The concept of the giant robot was to grow ever more important and what Harold Wilson, Prime Minister of another small island remaking its industrial base in a changed world, had called 'the white heat of technology' was shaping anime along with the rest of Japanese society. Tezuka's genius had given the anime industry a flying start. In 1965, the man who would take the giant robot genre in a new direction, and integrate Japanese folklore yet more closely into the heart of anime, started his career. Nagai Go would become the robot's most exciting new exponent.

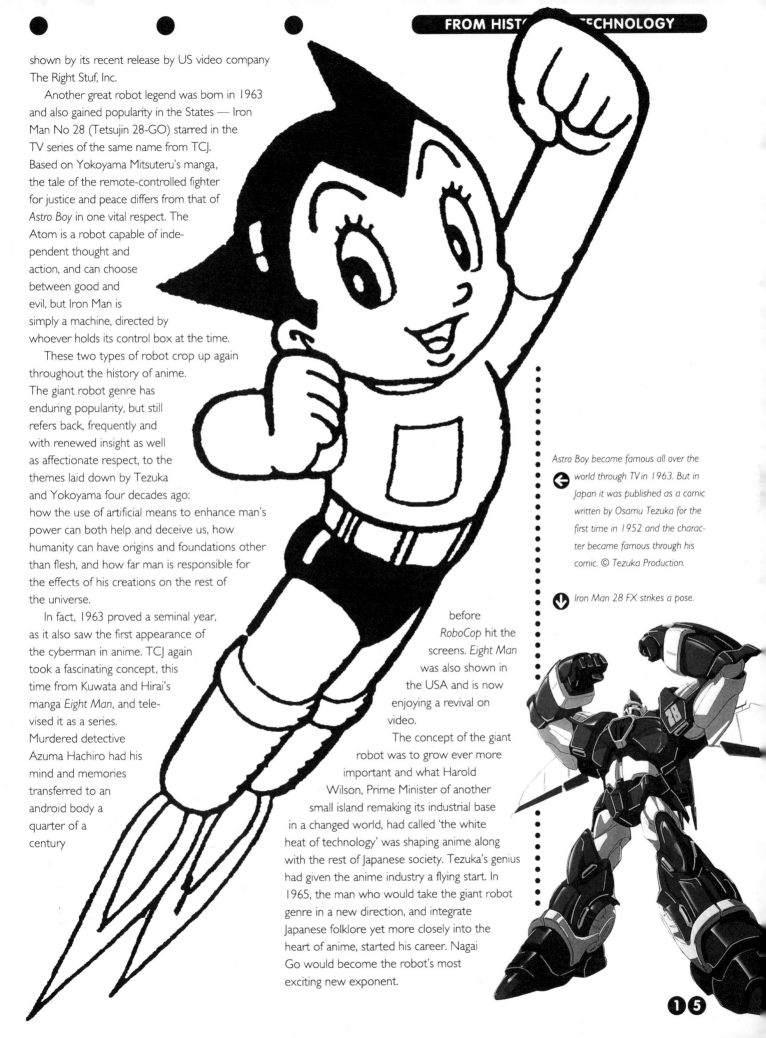

Astro Boy became famous all over the world through TV in 1963. But in Japan it was published as a comic written by Osamu Tezuka for the first time in 1952 and the character became famous through his comic. © Tezuka Production.

Iron Man 28 FX strikes a pose.

from robots to cyberpunk

THE SEVENTIES AND BEYOND

2

Nagai Go started his career as a manga artist in 1965, as assistant to one of the field's greats, Ishinomori Shotaro, and by 1970 was already established as a superstar of the manga and anime industries. Starting in humour manga, he soon developed other themes — his abiding interest in the supernatural and Japanese folklore led to a stream of productions showing this influence, of which the most famous is certainly *Devilman*, in his own view his most important work.

In October 1972, Nagai first produced *Mazinger Z* for *Shonen Jump* comic, and the animated series appeared on Fuji TV just two months later. *Mazinger Z* introduced a new element to the robot. It postulated a physiological, almost psychic link between the machine and its pilot. Either the robot's creator or the robot itself 'chose', or was 'linked by fate' to, its youthful companion, who steered it through a series of breathtaking adventures, fighting evil and defeating the enemies of mankind. This unique companionship was not without its price — the pilot's own body could feel every attack on the robot, and his new dedication to the cause of justice sometimes created problems in his everyday life and relationships with friends.

High technology, high adventure and control over the kind of powerful machine any teenager would love to own was already a strong combination, and the emotional bonding added by

Devilman *(© Nagai Go/Dynamic* ↗ *Planning).*

↘ *Nagai Go (© Dynamic Planning).*

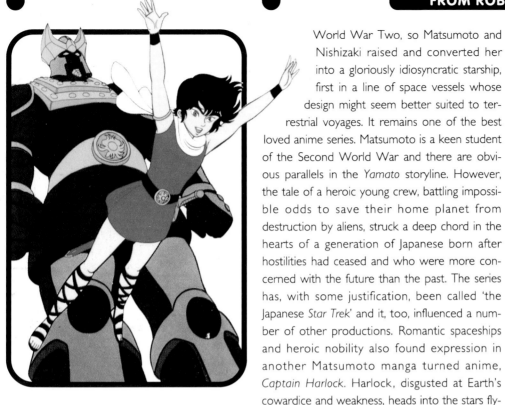

Nagai proved irresistible. *Mazinger Z* was followed by *Great Mazinger*, *God Mazinger*, *Steel Robot Jeeg*, *Grandizer*, *God Mars*, *Starvengers* and a host of others, many from artists developing Nagai's theme. The popularity of the giant robot seemed unending, and the colourful and original designs, often with overtones of samurai armour and weaponry, lent themselves to merchandising so well that the toys began to make inroads into Western markets.

Another great anime legend was born in 1974 when Matsumoto Reiji and Nishizaki Yoshinobu's mighty series *Space Battleship Yamato* first set sail. The real *Yamato* was sunk in

World War Two, so Matsumoto and Nishizaki raised and converted her into a gloriously idiosyncratic starship, first in a line of space vessels whose design might seem better suited to terrestrial voyages. It remains one of the best loved anime series. Matsumoto is a keen student of the Second World War and there are obvious parallels in the *Yamato* storyline. However, the tale of a heroic young crew, battling impossible odds to save their home planet from destruction by aliens, struck a deep chord in the hearts of a generation of Japanese born after hostilities had ceased and who were more concerned with the future than the past. The series has, with some justification, been called 'the Japanese *Star Trek*' and it, too, influenced a number of other productions. Romantic spaceships and heroic nobility also found expression in another Matsumoto manga turned anime, *Captain Harlock*. Harlock, disgusted at Earth's cowardice and weakness, heads into the stars flying the Jolly Roger from the stern of his spacegoing galleon, the *Arcadia*, in the 1977 film and TV series bearing his name.

Meanwhile, other themes continued to be developed, and sports, soap opera, fairytale and legend all had their place. One of the most popular and enduring anime characters, Lupin III, a cheerful thief-cum-ladykiller, made his début in 1971 and is still going strong today. Lupin's 'gang' were a not entirely honest but still united version of the 'character team', another popular anime theme, especially in TV series. The stress placed by Japanese society on teamwork is reflected in numerous productions about youthful groups

God Mazinger — *the robot and pilot*
 Yamato Hino.

The God Mazinger *team*

Mars, pilot of the giant robot
⬆ *God Mars.*

working together for a cause (usually the defence of the planet and the overthrowing of evil), finding one of its finest expressions in the first series of *Gatchaman* in 1972. This hugely popular series was butchered by a succession of American editors for US screening, but remained strong enough to add a legion of Western fans to its Japanese following and retains a large audience today. Five young people, each with his or her own problems, quirks and talents, combined to make a deadly fighting force against Earth's foes.

Just as the seventies started with a new twist on the giant robot, the decade also ended that way. The initial driving force on this occasion was writer Tomino Yoshiyuki, and the vehicle was his creation *Mobile Suit Gundam*, a huge saga composed of TV series, films and OAVs which is still in production today, with a new TV series airing

at the beginning of 1993. Tomino's robots were simply machines, incapable of independent thought, like Tetsujin 28-GO, but he didn't totally abandon the concept of 'psychic linkage' between robot and pilot. Instead, he transformed it into a new type of human ability; an extraordinary affinity for technology combined with psychic powers, including the capacity to communicate empathically with others who share that ability. Those possessed of this power are NewTypes. The technologies of *Gundam* were rooted at or beyond the leading edge of scientific possibility, but its characters, powerful and vulnerable at once, still played out the old dramas of love and hate, betrayal and revenge, death and survival. The new robot designs were solid, convincing and eminently marketable, making the *Gundam* saga one of the most successful series, both in terms of merchandising and longevity.

Gundam's success ushered in a new wave of robot series, and the early eighties proved a boom period for TV anime of all kinds. Masters like Tezuka, Nagai and Miyazaki were still producing powerful work, but new talents also appeared, including Takahashi Rumiko, the most successful female manga artist in Japan. Her

Urusei Yatsura, which made its TV début in 1981, told the tale of high school romance between girl crazy Moroboshi Ataru and alien princess Lum. This blend of sf, comedy and high weirdness is still one of the most popular series today. Keeping up the comedic tone, Toriyama Akira's manga and TV series Dr Slump & Aralechan introduced us to the world of Penguin Village, home

Alien princess Lum from Urusei Yatsura.

Lum and reluctant fiance Ataru Moroboshi.

of mad inventor Dr Slump and his 'little girl', the terrifyingly loud and persistent robot Arale.

In 1982, when *Macross* (*Super Dimensional Fortress Macross*) hit Japan's TV screens, another giant robot legend was born, along with the quintessential idol singer, ultrabimbo Lyn Minmay. The teenager with dreams of becoming a singing star became the idol of millions, and designer Mikimoto Haruhiko's misty, sensual watercolours depicting Minmay in various romantic poses appeared on bedroom and study walls all over Japan. The plot importance and fan popularity of the show's robot weapons, especially the transforming Valkyries, has never obscured the far greater impact of the characters on *Macross*'s young audience.

Minmay's fame grew even further when, in the mid-eighties, American company Harmony Gold asked producer Carl Macek to find a Japanese animated series for US TV syndication. Unable to locate a series which conformed either in number of episodes or cultural acceptability to the requirements of the American public as he saw them, Macek took three different and unrelated series (*Macross*, *Southern Cross* and *Mospeada*), re-wrote and re-edited them, and created *Robotech*. This became one of the most popular US animated series, and was widely shown in Europe.

Television was still the major medium for anime, although 1983 saw the birth of a vital new element — the OAV, or Original Animation Video. OAVs are produced specifically for release on video, without prior TV or film scheduling. The OAV is a useful means of distributing less widely popular types of programming, or those which would have difficulty getting onto television, especially erotica. With the changing economics of TV production during the eighties and the widespread use of home video hardware, the OAV grew in importance, and in today's less

Living up to their 'official' codename, the Lovely Angels and feline side-kick Mughi.

 *Yuri at work.*

The Dirty Pair spring into action...

That's Kei behind the shades.

Kei and Yuri at the controls of the
⬆ *hardy Angel.*

Dirty Pair: Project Eden, a cyberpunk
➡ *romp with Kei and Yuri in fighting*
form.

expansive times it is the major medium for new anime production. The softporn OAV series *Cream Lemon* began production in 1983, although it was preceded by the first part of the enjoyable but unremarkable hard-sf story *Dallos*.

The OAV market expanded rapidly, although film and TV anime continued to thrive. 1983 saw the cinema release of *Nausicaa of the Valley of the Wind*, Miyazaki Hayao's film based on his own manga (later released in the USA and UK with over twenty minutes cut out, on Vestron Video, as *Warriors of the Wind*). With years of television experience behind him, Miyazaki's lyrical imagination found its true expression in feature films. He has continued to produce magnificent movies, staking a strong claim to be one of the foremost current Japanese directors.

The other main film event of 1983 passed almost unnoticed — except among those who saw the film *Crushers* and began to ask questions about a tantalisingly brief filmclip seen on one of the screens in the background of a scene. Who were those two girls? What were they doing? The questions were asked so often that in 1985 *Crushers* creator Takachiho Haruki and Sunrise answered with the début of the Dirty Pair. Kei and Yuri, codenamed Lovely Angels but given their other name — usually behind their backs — because of the number of disasters which followed in their wake, appeared in OAVs and films, followed Lyn Minmay onto the walls of every Japanese teenager's bedroom, made the leap to Europe and America, and are now loved by anime fans everywhere. With their irrepressible energy, good humour and minuscule working outfits, they were made for stardom.

Kei and Yuri work for the World's Welfare Work Association (commonly known as 3WA) as a sort of cross between secret agent and social worker. 3WA exists to solve your problems — at a price; governments having trouble with leakage of secrets, companies whose technology is being transferred without their consent, even individuals can have a team of highly trained and experienced individuals sort out their difficulties for a fat fee. When the Trouble Consultants assigned are the Dirty Pair, however, there's also a massive excess to be paid on your insurance claim for property damage, injury and loss of life. In their spaceship the Lovely Angel, aided and abetted by a giant furry genetic construct called Mughi, the Dirty Pair go after bad guys and good times with gusto.

In many eyes, though, all this is still the prelude

to the main event. Despite everything — the humour, the intelligence, the history, the psychology, the action, the adventure, the lyricism, the erotica, the huge accumulation of technical skills over seventy years of film-making — in the eyes of most British critics, Japanese animation arrived from outer darkness in one cataclysmic explosion at the beginning of the nineties with the first British showing of Otomo Katshuhiro's film of his manga *Akira*. The arrival in Britain of this dazzling, assured box of fireworks, released in Japan in July 1988 and one of over 200 anime films, OAVs and TV series premièred that year, is, as you may recall, where this brief history began.

Anime continues to flourish in its native land. TV is less vital to the medium since the rise of the OAV, but there are still many new TV series in production and classics are frequently screened — in 1992 there were almost thirty hours of anime on TV every week in Tokyo. Video has brought new talent into the field and film is still important — one of the biggest-grossing films of 1992 was Miyazaki's latest anime release, *Porco Rosso*.

However, the sad loss of Tezuka Osamu, who died of stomach cancer in 1989, left a gap no-one else could fill; the anime and manga industry had lost its father figure. Nevertheless, many other greats of the seventies and early eighties are still active, creative forces — people like Miyazaki, Nagai, Tomino and Takahashi. Manga is still a potent breeding ground for new anime, but has been joined by computer games; once simply another way to merchandise successful concepts, these are beginning to develop as a point of origin for concepts later turned into video or film.

Ever since the early years of the century, there have been new ways to tell the old stories. The medium may be film, video, the printed word or a computer programme; the stories remain the same. Anime, before, during and after *Akira*, is one of Japan's most powerful narrative languages. Now we're listening, too.

The Japanese video cover for Flight 005
 Conspiracy.

3 sci-fi anime

Japan is the biggest consumer of science fiction in the world, and work by Western writers is as eagerly read as that of local authors. Naturally, anime reflects this, with productions based on both manga and books from Japan and Western sources, often showing the influence of Western sf films like *Blade Runner*, *Terminator* and the *Alien* series. Most of the anime commercially available in Britain falls into what might loosely be described as the sf/fantasy category, but there's a great deal more variety in sf anime than we have seen so far, both in style and in substance.

In the West, animation has taken only tentative steps into science fiction. In Japan, it rules the visual sf universe. There are sf live-action films and TV shows produced in Japan, but they are fewer and generally create less of a stir than their anime counterparts. The live-action movie *Gunhed*, with its one central giant robot in a rusting intelligent installation, has a long way to go to challenge the multiple mobile suits of *MS Gundam*, or the immense star-spanning fleets of *Legend of Galactic Heroes*, and no live-action director has yet managed the hackneyed old anime trick of having the mobile suit transform in midbattle into a striker aircraft or motorbike, without once disturbing the pilot's grip on the controls.

Orguss (*Super Dimensional Century Orguss*) is an

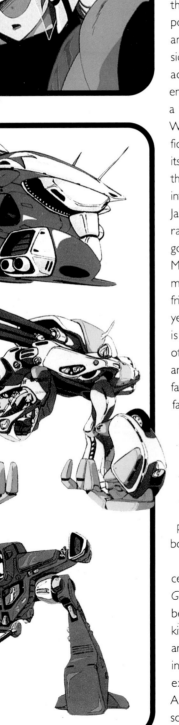

excellent example of the classic science fiction anime TV show. Produced by Mukaitsubu Toshitsuku for TMS in 1983, it features characters designed by the brilliant young Mikimoto Haruhiko, already famous for his work on *Super Dimensional Fortess Macross* a year earlier. The story of young pilot Katsuragi Kei, catapulted by the misuse of a powerful weapon into an alternate dimension where he finds adventure, experience and love, is of a type familiar in Western science fiction. *Orguss* uses its dimensional gate theory to throw together intelligent alternate dinosaur Jabby; the peaceable trading race the Emaan (including gorgeous seventeen year-old Mimsy) and their mortal enemies the Terram; Kei's oldest friend Olsen, who landed five years short of Kei in time and is already well established on the other side when Kei joins the Emaan; and the daughter Kei had unwittingly fathered the night before he left on his fateful last mission. Apart from its gentle humour and human relationships, the series is best remembered for its mecha, the mighty Orguss and opposing Nikick. The series sold millions of toys and kits throughout Japan — and since the largely female Emaan ship's crew included female pilots, there were toys for the girls as well as the boys.

However, all other robot merchandising success pales beside the achievement of *Mobile Suit Gundam* and its related series and films. It's been estimated that there are ten *Gundam* kits in existence for every man, woman and child in Japan. This indicates only indirectly the power the series still exerts over Japanese anime fans. Although the original *MS Gundam* series was screened in 1979 and the animation now looks very dated, the characters still feature regularly in

Previous page: *The Orguss mecha in three of its modes, plus Kei Katsuragi, the hero of Orguss.*

Kei in jubilant mood.

Orguss *mecha.*

Kei's daughter Athena.

reader polls and articles in current Japanese anime magazines. As recently as 1988 a feature film, *Char's Counterattack (Kido Senshi v Gundam: Gyakushu No Char)* was still recounting what might — or might not — be the final chapter in the personal battle of the 1979 series' earnest hero Amuro Ray and charismatic blond antihero Char Aznable. Many other characters in the *Gundam* universe, both old and new, are still as popular as ever. There are novels and manga, magazines and books, and literally countless fanzines, all based on the *Gundam* saga.

On one level, *Gundam* is the ultimate space opera. It has been compared to *Star Wars*; there are certainly conceptual similarities between creator Tomino Yoshiyuki's NewTypes and the Lucas concepts of the Force and the Jedi mythology, and feisty girls in the Princess Leia mould occur in multiples in *MS Gundam*. Tomino avoids

the difficulties experienced by many sf films, in which action either takes place between large fleets over great distances with little individual involvement or is rooted in one restricted area with a very small group of characters and consequent loss of scale. Instead, he uses vast spacefleets and yet retains the human drama of individual pilots engaged in hand-to-hand combat in mobile suits at the centre of the action by means of pseudo-scientific jiggery-pokery. The robots and big guns are fast, exciting and glossy, but they share equal billing, and often concede first place, to the fascinating stories of the large group of characters round whom he builds his web of sub-plots. While the galaxy has to be saved, people still bribe, plot, fall in and out of love, and struggle to cope with life and work.

 *Kei and robot girl Mohm.*

Kei and Mimsy Lars.

Space Fantasia R2001: a colony ship.

Space Fantasia R2001: space colony.

Mankind leaves Earth seeking a new home among the stars.

The sheer quality of story construction and character design in *Gundam* is the reason it has outlasted its competition and remains a great favourite with the fans. Its enduring success gives the lie to the idea that robot shows onlylast as long as the toy ranges they sell remain in fashion. If the characters and concepts were not so enduring, a part of a whole generation's youth, the merchandise would not continue to sell. The high quality of *Gundam* has given longevity to its merchandising, and not vice versa.

Science fiction anime isn't only set in the far future. The general level of interest in robotics, technological gadgetry and so on encourages the production of stories like *Black Magic M(ario): 66*, in which a powerful humanoid seek-and-destroy robot is accidentally unleashed on a city not unlike modern Tokyo, and both hunts and is hunted in a gripping hide-and-seek, chase-and-evade story whose ending is genuinely nervewracking. A strong, attractive female reporter in the Sigourney Weaver/Ripley mould is the central character — just one example of the numerous female characters in sf anime who play strong, leading roles. In a more comic vein, *Metal Skin Panic Madox – 01* tells the story of an ordinary guy who just wants to be on time for a date with his girlfriend, but manages to get caught up in a terrifying shoot-out between powered armour suits in the streets, shopping malls and car parks of another contemporary city. Back in the hard-sf mould, the 1987 OAV *Space Fantasia R2001*, based on a popular manga, looks at the problems of space colonisation in the not-too-distant-future.

Japan being the most technophiliac country on Earth, it's not surprising cyberpunk is so popular there. The genre, defined for the West by William Gibson and Bruce Sterling, has found a home in anime and manga, where many writers and designers have used its style and some have absorbed its substance as part of the cultural mix from which anime draws. *Cyber City Oedo 808* is a three part OAV series whose bleak, corrupt city and alien-

Previous page: *Priss, dynamic heroine of Bubblegum Crisis.*

Metal Skin Panic Madox – 01: title
 mecha.

Priss, suited up and ready to rock
 'n' roll.

dreams of rock stardom, but also wants freedom and peace of mind; Linna Yamazaki, whose attempts to make a career as an entertainer have not met with great success, wants a goal in life and somewhere to belong; and Nene Romanova, computer wizard and runaway, needs to escape her restrictive upbringing and live her life in her own way.

The series is sometimes

ated characters combine cyberpunk's core themes with influences from Western films like *RoboCop* and elements from horror movies, even the dark romance of the true High Gothic vampire tale. The OAV series *Bubblegum Crisis* is set in a devastated future Tokyo, where a wicked and dangerous corporation is out to control the whole city by the use of fearsome cybercreatures, and is dominated by four females in the sharpest body-armour ever designed. Sonoda Ken-ichi, one of Japan's leading chara designers, created Sylia, Priss, Linna and Nene, the Knight Sabers, a group of vigilante fighters pitted against the Genom Corporation and cybercrime, who power through a series of fastpaced adventures on a tide of hightech weaponry and rock music.

Even here, the human element dominates. *Bubblegum Crisis* focuses as strongly on the development of the relationships between the team and their personal growth as it does on the armoured martial arts ballet in which they engage in each episode. All four characters change and question their own beliefs as the series progresses. Sylia Stingray, the team's founder and leader, is trying to avenge her murdered father and the misuse of his life's work; Priss Asagiri, the number one fighter,

described, unfairly, as 'babes in battlesuits'. It offers more than that stereotyped dismissal implies. The four lead characters are strong without being hard; powerful and feminine women who are not afraid to take risks. Its cyberpunk surface gloss can't mask its old fashioned qualities of strong stories, well-developed characters and action-packed, fast-paced entertainment. It's certainly one of the best anime productions currently available in Britain.

Cyberpunk and horror elements in anime aren't confined only to science fiction stories. Fantasy anime also has plenty of room for both.

worlds of fantasy

 Devilman *and Silene (© Nagai Go/ Dynamic Planning).*

A huge, organic looking robot flies on gossamer wings over a dense, ancient forest, folding the wings under a carapace like a giant insect's as it lands. Fluttering out of its control cabin comes a tiny creature — winged, feminine, exquisite — a fairy. Deep in the well lurk water sprites. Welcome to the most unlikely of giant robot series, Tomino Yoshiyuki's *Aura Battler Dunbine*.

It's sometimes difficult to separate fantasy from science fiction. The two genres share many elements and cover much the same ground. However, anime certainly has a strong tradition of the purely fantastic, rooted in Japanese folk-lore but borrowing both ancient and modern elements from the rest of the world, as well as from more traditional folkloric or pseudohistori-cal fantasies. There are part-human or seemingly human creatures, like the spider-female in *Supernatural Beast City* (released as *Monster City* in the USA), and evil spirits or ghosts in innocent guise, such as the infant girl demon in the shad-owlands of *Hell City Shinjuku*. The Lucifer Hawks of *Silent Moebius*, Asamiya Kia's 'cyber psychic movie' (which has so far appeared as a manga series and two related films), take many forms based on a combination of traditional elements and ideas borrowed from such influential Western movies as *Alien*.

When Bram Stoker wrote *Dracula* in 1897, there was a broad consensus among his reader-

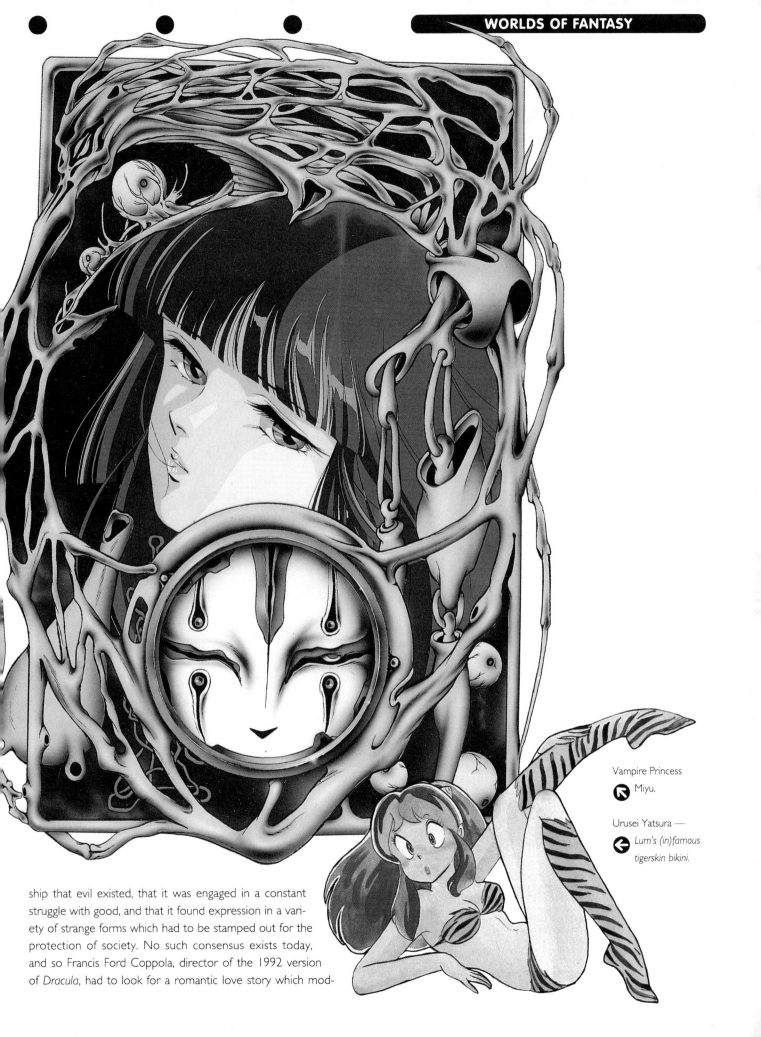

Vampire Princess
Miyu.

Urusei Yatsura —
Lum's (in)famous
tigerskin bikini.

ship that evil existed, that it was engaged in a constant
struggle with good, and that it found expression in a variety of strange forms which had to be stamped out for the
protection of society. No such consensus exists today,
and so Francis Ford Coppola, director of the 1992 version
of *Dracula*, had to look for a romantic love story which mod-

Urusei Yatsura

ern audiences could understand as Dracula's main motivation. In Japan, however, producers know that high school and undergraduate audiences can accept such stories as *Vampire Princess Miyu*, in which a female vampire tries to protect schoolchildren from attacks by others of her kind while a professional psychic investigator, suspicious of her motives, hinders her efforts. Miyu is guarded by a protective demon, but the dangers she encounters often threaten to overcome them both. Simple artefacts of childhood, redolent of innocence, such as dolls and marionettes, become menacing creatures of evil, and the whole fabric of everyday life is permeated with the supernatural.

Many other fantasy anime productions also feature traditional ghost story and folktale elements, some seriously — for example, Nagai Go's *Devilman* — and some in a comical sense, in series like *Kitaro Gegege*. Here, a young boy with psychic powers travels round Japan fighting supernatural forces with a motley crew of ghosts and spirits, including a flying blanket, a piece of paper and a cowardly, greedy ghost with the face of a ferret and an uncanny ability to scrounge food.

More familiar to Western eyes is the kind of fantasy found in the many anime inspired by computer console games or roleplaying games (RPG). Anything with 'dragon' in the title may well have a console connection, and one popular OAV series, the thirteen part *Record of Lodoss War*, grew out of what is probably Japan's best-known homegrown RPG scenario and has all the classic elements of *Dungeons and Dragons* at its best. There's a copybook party of adventurers (consisting of fighter, dwarf, wizard, thief, cleric and phenomenally cute elfgirl), a heroic and noble king and his paladins to be the good guys, a dark and wicked empire as the opposition, a well designed medieval-style setting and a wide range of interesting supporting characters includ-ing, of course, dragons.

Much of Takahashi Rumiko's work is in the field of fantasy or sf/fantasy. One of the richest women in Japan thanks to her many popular manga creations, she specialises in stories which put a fantastic twist on everyday life. Her best known creation is *Urusei Yatsura* (generally trans-lated as *Those Obnoxious Aliens*), in which alien princess Lum, with awesome powers and equally awesome tigerskin bikini, falls in love with lecher-ous student Moroboshi Ataru and comes to live in Tomobiki Town. *Urusei Yatsura* is one of the most popular anime productions. Like much of Takahashi's work, it has strong elements of soap opera in its romantic-comedy stories, as Lum and her many alien or supernatural friends cre-ate chaos in the peaceful life of the town. The TV series and films are packed with hilarious incidents; for example, *Angry Sherbet* has

Lum's greedy girlfriend, and just about everyone else within range, under air attack from a self-renewing horde of enraged ice-cream cones after her moneymaking scheme goes disastrously wrong.

Ranma ¹/₂, an everyday tale of martial arts, high school romance and magically induced changes of sex and species caused by immersion in water, is also hugely popular. Saotome Ranma has an unusual problem — he turns into she (redheaded and immensely cute) when imm-ersed in cold water, and only hot water can turn him back. Saotome senior is similarly afflicted — he turns into a giant panda. A number of other characters in the series also have odd reactions to immer-sion in water, and most of them are kept busy by falling madly in love with the wrong people and holding fierce martial arts battles.

In recent years, Takahashi's enormous gift for wacky comedy has gone hand-in-hand with a darker, more macabre vein in her writing, as evinced in some of the titles in her

Urusei Yatsura — *Ataru falling for Lum again.*

Cagliostro Castle — the dastardly Count looms over Lupin, Clarice and the gang.

Ishikawa Goemon shows his samurai blood.

Rumic World series of manga and OAVs, like *The Laughing Target* and *Fire Tripper*. To many of her Western fans, the idea that she is an exponent of the Japanese horror story, as firmly rooted in the darker side of her culture as Nagai Go, would seem unbelievable. However, her work is a demonstration of the power of fantasy, both dark and light, in Japanese storytelling in general and anime in particular.

The ultimate creator of fantasies in modern anime is Miyazaki Hayao. A career spanning over thirty years has given him a technical command of the medium which is almost unparalleled, and as a director he is one of Japan's greatest. In 1979, he gave notice of what was to come with *Cagliostro Castle*, starring that well known character Lupin III. The heroine Clarice, innocent, heroic and charming, is the prototype for every ingénue in later Miyazaki films; and the setting is that perfect dream of middle-Europe 'as it never was, but should have been', which he later employed to such good effect in *Kiki's Delivery Service*. In *Cagliostro Castle* he achieved the difficult feat of taking a well-loved and renowned set of characters, making them his own, and yet not changing them out of recognition. He also found his own voice.

Working in partnership with longtime colleague Takahata Isao, his Nibariki and Studio Ghibli ventures have produced a string of beautifully crafted, poignant and compelling feature films throughout the eighties. After his ecofantasy *Nausicaa of the Valley of the Wind*, he took us into the skies over a mining community based on South Wales for *Laputa* in 1986, examining a young boy's dream of adventure and discovery and a young girl's search for her past. In 1988, he went on a journey into his own past to recreate a magical country childhood in 1950s Japan for *My Neighbour Totoro*; the next year he created a city by the sea for *Kiki's Delivery Service*, in which a teenager who just happens to be a witch has to learn to live as an independent young adult, with all the gains and losses involved in leaving childhood behind.

Lupin and Clarice.

The hapless Zenigata plots yet another doomed attempt to arrest his nemesis.

Oops! Reckless driving...

Most recently, in 1992, Miyazaki and Takahata's *Porco Rosso* was one of the summer's major successes. This magical flight over the Adriatic in the 1920s by a group that includes a fighter ace who has been turned into a pig, an American mercenary who dreams of movie stardom, a beautiful chanteuse whose heart has been broken once too often and a seventeen year-old girl as innocent as she is impulsive, is one of my favourite films. With the same deftness of touch as an old Cary Grant romantic comedy, a seemingly infallible eye for the perfect composition and a wonderful sense of narrative pacing, this film could stand in any company without shame.

True fantasy — the unfettered flight of the human imagination — is alive and well and living in Japan. In anime, it can have free and generous rein, and of course appears in many different genres and formats; children's anime is often fantasy-based, and much erotic or softporn anime is also fantastic in content and style. Even in such a gritty, realistic genre as the crime story, it's not always possible to keep things completely normal.

Lupin III — Lupin, Jigen and the opposition.

5 cops and robbers

Criminal activity and its detection has always been a popular subject. The Japanese, essentially a law-abiding nation, enjoy a good crime story, and there are plenty in anime, although often leavened with comedy, fantasy or other, lighter seasoning.

One of the most successful comedic criminal characters is based firmly on a European model. Lupin III (Lupin Sansei), created by manga artist Monkey Punch, is modelled on the leading character in a 1920s French novel, *Arsene Lupin — Gentilhomme-Voleur* (*Arsene Lupin — Gentleman-Thief*), by Maurice LeBlanc. Indeed, Monkey Punch has made his Lupin the grandson of that famous thief, living in approximately contemporary times, and though he is assumed to be a citizen of Japan, his adventures span the globe. He is addicted to food, pretty girls, skintight trousers and crepe soles, and is a master of disguise. Lupin is aided and abetted by both Daisuke Jigen, an ace shot who grew up in Chicago, fled to Japan after some trouble with the mobs, liked it and stayed on, and Ishikawa Goemon, descendant of a famous samurai-thief and still stoically loyal to the old samurai codes. Mine Fujiko, a gor-

Previous page. Top: Lupin III: *Daisuke Jigen.* Bottom: *Lupin — an alternative mode of transport.*

 Lupin III: *Zenigata.*

Space Adventure Cobra: *Cobra and* *android aide Lady.*

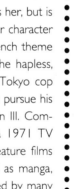

Cobra: *the Cobra Girls are as* *renowned as the Bond girls.*

geous but unreliable fellow-criminal who works with or against Lupin as the fancy takes her, but is his real love interest, is another regular character in his adventures. To continue the French theme there is even a Clouseau clone — the hapless, hopeless Inspector Zenigata, a good Tokyo cop who eventually transfers to Interpol to pursue his life's work of just failing to catch Lupin III. Commencing his anime adventures in a 1971 TV series, Lupin has starred on TV, in feature films and even a live-action series, as well as manga, and his adventures have been animated by many of the great names in the industry.

A criminal created and animated by just one artist, and in a totally different setting from Lupin, is Terasawa Buichi's Cobra from *Space Adventure Cobra.* The accent remains on lighthearted comic thrills. Again a popular manga character, Cobra began his anime career in the 1982 film, with the series *Space Cobra* beginning its TV run in the same year. Heavily influenced by the James Bond films, though the hero is more of a rough diamond, Cobra's adventures mix interplanetary crime and chicanery with girls human, alien and android. Terasawa has an acute eye for the offbeat detail and his mecha and settings, though always fantastic and often improbable in the extreme, always look convincing.

Bringing crime into a more everyday setting,

⬆ Cat's Eye: *Hitomi and Toshiro.*

➡ Golgo 13: *The Duke at work.*

two very popular series, *City Hunter* and *Cat's Eye*, are set in modern Tokyo. Both based on manga by Tsukasa Hojo, they also share a sense of style, considerable slickness of animation and a penchant for slapstick humour, particularly in the later series of *City Hunter* where the heroine's pursuit of the hero with an outsize hammer to repress any overt displays of lechery becomes a running gag. In the first series, screened in 1987, there's a slightly more serious tone. Ryo Saeba plies his trade as a hired gun who can be contacted by leaving a message addressed with the letters XYZ at the information point at Shinjuku Station. Even when the humour overtakes the action, *City Hunter* is still a fast, exciting romp.

The first series of *Cat's Eye* was screened four years earlier, in 1983. Three sisters, Ai, Rui and Hitomi, keep the popular Cat's Eye coffee house and moonlight as art thieves of incomparable cheek and skill. Their father has disappeared, and the objects they steal all came from his collection or had a connection with him; they are stealing not for profit but in the hope of uncovering those responsible, hoping to learn their motives.

A grittier, colder look at criminal activity is found in Dezaki Osamu's 1983 film *Golgo 13*. The title character, also known as 'Duke', is one of the most successful comic characters; the manga of the same title, created by Saito Takao, has been running since 1969. *Golgo 13* is a contract killer — cynical, ruthless and calculating. The film focuses on one particular job, the killing of the recently married son of a gangland boss. It's successfully carried out, but the killer himself becomes a target. It seems the father of his victim is so hell-bent on revenge that he even offers his widowed daughter-in-law to a crazed psychotic as an incentive to go after the Duke. But the case isn't quite as simple as it seems. With many elements, and some stylistic tricks, in common with sixties Western spy thrillers, *Golgo 13* (released in the USA by Streamline Pictures as *The Professional*) is darker and nastier than most.

Can you imagine *Hill Street Blues* with robots as well as patrol cars? Masami Yuuki did, and in 1988 the Headgear team brought his dream to life as the seven part OAV series *Patlabor* (*Kido Keisatsu Patlabor*). Heavily supported by leading anime magazine *NewType*, *Patlabor* was a huge success and became the first OAV to be picked up as a TV series, leading to a second series, a feature film and a music video. There's a new feature film in production for release late in 1993. A new lease of life for the team show concept and the giant robot genre in one cunningly engineered package, *Patlabor* has everything — an idiosyncratic and likeable team of characters, from redheaded rookie heroine Izumi Noa to loudmouthed, aggressive and deeply insecure veteran Ota Isao; a near contemporary setting in the Tokyo of 1998, with many of its street scenes and backgrounds recognisable as survivors from the late 1980s; the whole fabulous range of stories available in any city, from the mythically comic — giant albino alligators in the sewers of Tokyo — to the deeply serious — crooked arms salesmen testing out new product on the streets; and last, but never least, the magnificent INGRAM operational mobile suits, or LABORs as the series calls them, the most breathtaking step up from the panda car any police force is ever likely to make. As with the *Gundam* saga, though, the main element of *Patlabor*'s enduring success is not simply the mecha, but the developing relationships between its characters and their personal growth and changes.

In many cop shows, both Western and Japanese, the police are portrayed as flatfoots doing their best with hopelessly inadequate financial and intellectual resources. Not so in Masamune Shirow's ecological comedy *Dominion*, made in 1989 and released on Manga Video three years later. The police force in Newport City are a bunch of homicidal maniacs whose methods of interrogation range from playing grenade golf with suspects as the holes, to tying them to a spinning wheel as targets for a knife-throwing contest in a crazy gameshow parody. The local population often suffer more at the hands of the defenders of law and order than the criminal fraternity. The Tank Police bring to their

work a lunatic *esprit de corps* and enthusiasm, but the criminals still have the best weaponry, including grenades which explode into giant, multi-coloured, roadblocking dildos and a pair of genetically engineered catgirls whose clothes are considerably smaller than their armaments.

One interesting aspect of the anime crime or cop show — and indeed of anime in general — is that the female protagonist is neither a rarity nor an oddity. The pull of women in uniform, or toting heavy weaponry, is a well known element of male fantasy, but as in *Bubblegum Crisis*, the women in *Patlabor* or *Cat's Eye* don't just decorate, they act. Films like *Golgo 13* take the conventional Western view that weaker parties are there to be abused, but the women in *Golgo 13* are subjected to no worse levels of violence than the male characters. Elsewhere, even in such outrageous parodies as *Dominion*, the treatment handed out to female characters is often better than that offered in Western live-action.

Golgo 13: *Duke, Cindy and* *Bregan.*

Cat's Eye: *Rui, Hitomi and Ai.*

children's hour

Hello Spank!: Aiko and
↘ Spank.

Spank in a sticky
↓ situation.

Anime for young children — say, up to the age of ten or eleven — often originates as a TV series, and there is less connection with manga than in adult titles, most very young viewers being fairly new to the comic buying habit. Toys and games, especially the tiny, cheap sweet-and-toy combinations on sale in every Japanese sweetshop, reinforce the popularity of their favourite characters for the very young. There are, however, several magazines devoted to children's TV, like *Terebi-Kun* (which is most closely translated as *TV Friend*), which feature popular live-action and anime charas in manga strips, starting the process which can lead to a lifelong manga involvement.

The same mix of school and home-life stories, retelling of classic tales, fairy stories, slapstick and action/adventures that make up most Western children's programming can be found in anime. There is usually a strong, but not overtly intrusive, moral element to the story structure. Programmes are generally aimed to appeal to either boys or girls, but girls' stories often contain as much action and adventure as boys', and boys' stories often have strong, positive female characters as well as the expected young heroes.

There has been so much anime produced for children that it would be difficult to do it justice even in a book

My Patraasche: *Patraasche and his young saviour Jehan.*

Twins at St Clare's: *the girls plot some mischief.*

entirely devoted to the subject. A few examples will have to serve as an indicator of the vast scope.

One typical 'everyday life' story is *Hello Spank!* (*Ohayo Spank!*), a TV series and film about a little girl called Aiko and her puppy, Spank. Aiko's father was lost at sea many years ago and her mother is working abroad, so Aiko goes to live with her uncle in a seaside town. Her puppy is run over, but out of the blue Spank arrives to turn her life upside down with his almost human antics. With the help of this most unusual dog, Aiko faces all the problems and changes involved in growing up.

More recently, *Little Miss Maruko* (*Chibi Maruko-Chan*) has been one of the most unexpected successes on TV. The story is simply the daily life of a ten year-old girl in a Japanese school. Its deliberately simplistic animation and storylines, basic to the point of banality, have baffled many Western fans — most of whom missed the point completely. Popular with chil-

dren, the series also strikes a chord in many adult women who can immerse themselves in a nostalgia for their own childhood and schooldays. Just like *Peanuts*, it brings home to adults, in subtle and comical style, the absolute powerlessness of children; it also gives children, through the reassurance that 'this happens to all of us sometimes', some help in living through that powerlessness.

Another kind of school story altogether is *Twins at St Clare's*. Many Western novels are adapted into anime for children — among them have been Stevenson's *Treasure Island*, Burnett's *The Secret Garden* and Alcott's *Little Women*. *Twins at St Clare's* comes from a book by Enid Blyton, whose continuing popularity among the young is the despair of politically correct librarians and teachers everywhere. Identical twins, forced to change schools, deliberately set out to cause havoc at their new boarding school until they gradually come to realise that they like St Clare's and want to stay there. Single-sex education is

My Patraasche: *the beautiful landscapes and depictions of old Antwerp make this a joy to watch.*

Mon Pe: *Mon-Mon wonders what's going on...*

Havoc in the nursery as PePe and her toys go on the march, with Mon-Mon in pursuit.

not the norm in Japan, but the idea of the British segregated boarding school is very popular in manga, and in anime found an expression in the comedy film/OAV series *Project A-KO*, aimed at a rather older audience than the twins' adventure and with much higher levels of havoc caused.

The series *My Patraasche*, taken from *A Dog of Flanders* by European romantic novelist Ouida, shows a different type of classic adaptation; more serious, more emotional and slower to develop its themes. Beautifully animated in a neo-realistic style, the story is set on the outskirts of Antwerp in the last century, in which a grandfather and his

grandson rescue an abused dog and earn his undying devotion.

Series like *Mon Pe* use fantasy to leaven the banality of children's everyday lives. PePe, baby daughter of unsuccessful writer Mr Kano (who lives in a dream world most of the time) and his fashion designer wife, has supernatural powers. Her parents aren't aware of this when they decide she needs a babyminder to keep her company, and hire a naïve fifteen year-old called Mon-Mon. She's a country girl, totally unsophisticated, who wants to be a fashion designer and sees a job in a designer's household as a dream come true. However, when she settles in and starts to notice strange things in the nursery — like PePe's stuffed toys walking and talking — she takes fright. PePe has become so attached to her that Mon-Mon stays on despite her misgivings, and light-hearted domestic chaos ensues.

A popular form of fantasy in anime — with many fans long passed the age of ten — is the 'magical princess' genre. The heroine, a magical creature in disguise, usually masquerades as an ordinary schoolgirl living with a typical Japanese family. She uses her powers to solve problems in everyday life, as in *Magical Princess Minky Momo*, where she changes into an eighteen year-old to handle situations beyond the capabilities of her usual ten year-old self or to take her friends on fantasy adventures. Minky Momo is probably the best known, but their numbers are legion. They are generally accompanied by one or more small, fluffy animal companion and usually dress in pink or a similar sugared-pastel shade. The young viewer identifies with the heroine, at one and the same time sweet, pretty and powerful.

Oddly enough, the equivalent boys' fantasy programmes usually feature a far less heroic and positive boy — often clumsy, lazy or stupid — as the figure for audience identification. He has a fantasy friend to help him with his problems, sometimes causing as many difficulties as he solves. One of the longest running of such series is *Doraemon*, in which the title character, a blue robot cat from the future, comes back in time to live with a particularly stupid and clumsy schoolboy and helps him cope with the problems he creates for himself.

Straight sf-adventure tales like *The Rescue Kids* (Lupin's creator Monkey Punch working for a younger audience) follow the format used so successfully in many other shows — a family working together, in this case in the family robot rental business, is threatened by an outside force, here an evil genius aiming for world

dominion with his 'destroid' robot. The two brothers and their sister, using all the resources of the family firm, band together to stop him. The usual family bickering and comic situations don't prevent the young viewer from picking up the moral points about the importance of teamwork and taking responsibility for the well being of the community.

The children who begin watching the adventures of *Anpan Man* (a superhero with a traditional bean-curd stuffed bun for a head) before they go to school don't all continue as lifelong anime and manga fans; but they contribute to the continuance of a culture which accepts anime and manga as part of the general spectrum of entertainment. If they wish, they can carry on through their teenage years with action, adventure and romance shows, science fiction and sports programmes, or even gourmet food shows and soap operas.

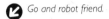

The Rescue Kids: *The kids can call on some weird and wonderful mecha to help their fight.*

Go and robot friend.

Ran.

and there's more... 7

井原西鶴

好色一代男

Based on the novel by IHARA SAIKAKU

THE SENSUALIST

OTHER TYPES OF ANIME

By now, you've probably gathered that the whole field of anime is a good deal wider than most British commentators would credit. The previous chapters have highlighted just a few of the topics anime covers. Here's a brief glimpse of a few more.

HISTORY

Japanese history is strongly represented in anime, as the numerous samurai/martial arts dramas and retellings of historical events, with or without elements of fantasy, testify. However, literary and social history is also a popular subject.

The Sensualist is based on a famous novel by poet and novelist Ihara Saikaku, first published in 1682, and tells the story of a young man of the merchant class who devotes his entire life to the pursuit of pleasure and erotic experience. Directed by Abe Yukio, it employs a huge range of experimental painting techniques to render the lush, exquisitely refined atmosphere of the pleasure quarters in which much of the book is set. The aesthetic of eroticism was of vital importance in seventeenth century Japan; the precise choice of kimono, the phrasing of a poem, the sight of a famous courtesan walking in the street with her entourage of servants and handmaidens, all were vital parts of the experience and just as important as — indeed more important than —

Previous page. *The Sensualist: the beautiful courtesan Komurasaki reads a letter.*

The Sensualist: *Komurasaki and merchant Yonosuke, the novel's hero.*

Komurasaki.

Merchant and courtesan.

Rose of Versailles: *Oscar de Jarjayes (the elegant blonde in uniform), Marie Antoinette and members of the court.*

Andre and Rosalie.

mere sex. *The Sensualist* conveys the highly stylised hothouse atmosphere of the place and period without neglecting the humanity of the characters involved.

Western history, too, is used as a basis for anime, and one enduringly popular TV series is *Rose of Versailles* (*Berusaiya No Bara*), screened in France, the land which inspired it, as *Lady Oscar*. The story tells of a beautiful young noblewoman, forced by circumstance to live disguised as a man at the court of Marie Antoinette and who falls in love with a soldier of the Revolution. *Rose of Versailles* combines romance, daring and glamour and proved popular both in Japan and Europe. Directed by Araki Shingo and Kawai Ken, the series was based on Ikeda Ryoko's manga and first screened in 1979.

SPORT

All kinds of sport are popular in anime — association football, ribbon gymnastics, boxing, martial arts, tennis, baseball, motor racing; all have films and series devoted to them. Baseball is the most popular foreign sport in Japan and, as well as being the centrepiece of series like Adachi Mitsuru's romantic drama *Touch* and films like the 1987 comedy-drama *Bats & Terry*, many characters in non-sports shows are glimpsed playing or watching it.

Boxing drama *The Champion* (*Ashita No Joe*) began with a seventy-nine episode TV series from Mushi Productions in 1979 and went on to a second series and two feature films. Its strong similarity to Stallone's boxing film series *Rocky* is even more in evidence in the Italian release title, *Rocky Joe*. A young orphan fights his way to the top, kills an opponent in the ring and retires, finally overcoming guilt and self doubt to make a bloody and triumphant comeback.

Women's sports have always been well-represented, and stories often focus on the difficulties of living a normal life around the demands of a sports career. Oka Hiromi, heroine of the 1973 tennis series *Aim for the Ace! (Ace O Nerae!)* starts her tennis career as a terrible player. Determination and the hard work of coach Munakata, who sees her potential when nobody else can, eventually pay off, and she not only becomes a top tennis player but wins the coach's heart. A film followed, and in 1988 the adventures of the still popular heroine from Yamamoto

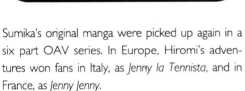

Sumika's original manga were picked up again in a six part OAV series. In Europe, Hiromi's adventures won fans in Italy, as *Jenny la Tennista*, and in France, as *Jenny Jenny*.

SOAP OPERA AND ROMANCE

Takahashi Rumiko's longrunning romantic fantasies *Urusei Yatsura* and *Ranma 1/2* are hugely popular, but she isn't the undisputed queen of this genre. Adachi Mitsuru's baseball romance *Touch*, premièred on TV in 1985 with a 101

episode series (which was followed by three films) and is still popular in Japan and Europe. The story of twin brothers, baseball fanatics in love with the same girl, touched a chord with Japanese teenagers in much the same way as *Neighbours* did in Britain. However, Takahashi has staked a strong claim to her place in the pantheon of pure soap opera, undiluted by sf or fantasy, with her longrunning series *Maison Ikkoku*. A young widow takes a job as manageress of a boarding house in a Japanese suburb, and through the everyday lives and problems of the various boarders a panorama unfolds of life in Japan in the early eighties, while the love of student Godai Yusaku for his landlady slowly develops. Will Kyoko ever be able to love again after the tragic loss of her young husband? Is Godai the right man for her? The Takahashi magic is at work again, proving that she doesn't need tigerskin bikinis or martial arts to hold the attention of her audience.

For pure soap opera sentiment, though, it's

The Champion: *young boxer Joe and friends Yoko, Danbei, Riki and Jose.*

Aim for the Ace!: *Hiromi takes on the champion Reika.*

Georgie: *Little Georgie and her adoptive family the Butmans.*

hard to beat series like the 1983 *Georgie* (*Lady Georgie*), whose forty-five episodes begin in Australia. Here, any similarity with other soaps shown in Britain ends. The time is the nineteenth century and the title character, a sweet blonde infant, is the orphan daughter of a criminal exiled to Australia, whose pregnant wife followed him and died soon after her baby was born. However, she first asked a kind passerby, Mr Butman, to take care of the child. The Butmans rear Georgie as sister to their own boys and determine never to tell her where she came from, but then Mr Butman is drowned and life becomes hard for the widow and her three children. A series of trials and tribulations in the best tradition of soap opera turns out right in the end.

SEX – WITH OR WITHOUT VIOLENCE

Sexual preferences or fantasies of any kind are not regarded as strange or reprehensible in Japan, where a long tradition of liberal thought has created an atmosphere in which anything is permissible in the privacy of your imagination. Anime provides a wide range of choices, from the mildly erotic to the frankly pornographic. Genitals are digitised or blacked out throughout, but this does nothing to disguise what's going on. There is a far wider acceptance of nudity than in the British media, and in shows aimed at young teenagers it is not uncommon to see characters in the shower or in various stages of undress. In general, sexual activity in anime is more restrained than in manga, but not always by a wide margin.

Urotsukidoji: Legend of the Overfiend and its follow-up, *Legend of the Demon Womb*, released on the Manga Video label in 1992 and 1993 respectively, would probably not be classed as erotica by most Japanese — it falls more easily into the category of apocalyptic sf/fantasy, and the overtly sexual elements, which are both violent and exploitative to both sexes, are simply another device by which the director and writer indicate the level of selfishness and amorality in individuals. The first film shows a destruction of the soul on a personal level reflecting the destruction of the whole of human morality, religion and philosophy as society finally breaks down under the weight of Armageddon. The second rehashes the Nazi survivor theme to indicate that evil calls itself by different names in different times, but is always essentially the same.

One aspect of sexuality in anime rarely touched on in Western entertainment is the issue of gender; rooted in Japan's long tradition of transvestism in entertainment, anime plays with the whole concept of gender in ways which few Western writers have ever attempted. Transsexuality, transvestism and variations on accepted sexual norms are not marginalised, and sometimes go centre stage, for example in *Mospeada* one of the heroes is a transvestite, in *3 x 3 Eyes* the hero works in a transvestite bar after school and has been partly brought up by the owner, and in *Joker Marginal City* the central character can switch genders seemingly at will.

THE SD PHENOMENON

Super Deformed charas and their variants have grown in popularity immensely since their introduction in the eighties, and console games are bringing them to audiences who have never heard of anime. Any kind of being — monster, supernatural creature, hero, villainous megalomaniac — can become an SD or CB chara, and any evil intent is translated into pure slapstick. Cute, squashed-down versions of existing charas and mecha are used principally in comedy and parody; original SD charas tend to be confined to console games. There are many SD manga and aniparo published, and in anime the best known are probably the manikins and mini-mecha of *SD Gundam*, a TV and OAV phenomenon which has now moved into areas of

its own, quite independent of the original *Gundam* storyline.

One of the most popular recent SD OAVs has been *Scramble Wars*, a Japanese *Wacky Races* featuring popular charas from *Bubblegum Crisis*, *Gall Force*, *Genesis Survivor Gaiarth* and other shows already blessed with an overabundance of cuteness. The Genom Corporation, in the original *Bubblegum Crisis* series a malevolent force out for world domination, is here sponsoring a cross-desert race which all the charas are out to win. If you've already seen the original shows, the script of *Scramble Wars* has lots of in-jokes to enjoy, but even if you haven't the sheer insane good humour will get to you in the end. And just to prove that it isn't just cute females who get even cuter in SD parodies, there's *CB Go Nagai World*, with sweet and innocent versions of Devilman and other normally terrifying wreakers of havoc from Nagai's world.

Anime has so many themes, stories and ideas to explore that this brief guide couldn't hope to contain them all...

Scramble Wars: *charas from* Bubblegum Crisis, Genesis Survivor Gaiarth *and* Ten Little Gall Force *fight it out for the* Genom Trophy.

anime in britain

Starfleet: *the crew of X-Bomber with lovely but mysterious Lamia and her furry guardian. (© Nagai Go/Dynamic Planning)*

Genesis Survivor Gaiarth: *Hero Ital and Sahari (in armour).*

Following page. Riding Bean: *Bean Bandit in action, and Bean with partner Rally Vincent.*

In 1991 Island World Communications (now Manga Entertainment Limited) released *Akira* on retail video, in both a dubbed version and a subtitled collectors' edition presented as a two-tape set with *The Making of Akira*. The outstanding success of both editions persuaded IWC that there was a market for anime, and in 1992 they launched their Manga Video label with Ashida Toyoo's *Fist of the North Star* — a feature length

version of a popular manga and anime TV series, *Hokuto No Ken*. The label released a total of eight tapes in its first year, and by early 1993 had expanded to include a further two labels — Ultra for Japanese live action and ICA for less mainstream films. Their plans include ventures into anime-linked computer games and other merchandise, and theatrical releases in major cities, whilst their name change reflects Manga Entertainment's commitment to anime in Britain.

Anime Projects has been set up to market the subtitled anime of US parent AnimEigo in Britain. So far their range has included the popular cyberpunk action series *Bubblegum Crisis* and fast-moving gangster tale *Riding Bean*, with many more releases planned from AnimEigo's large catalogue. The fan debate as to whether subbing or dubbing — either subtitles run under the action on screen or an English language voicetrack dubbed over the Japanese — is the better way to treat anime rages on, but there appears to be a demand for both.

Completing the roundup of anime labels in the UK, Western Connection, another small label, has released *The Sensualist*, an exquisite version of a seventeenth century Japanese novel about life in the pleasure quarters, and First International have re-released one of the great anime classics, albeit in a severely cut US version — *Warriors of the Wind*, the film version of Miyazaki Hayao's seminal environmental adventure manga *Nausicaa of the Valley of the Wind*. This wonderfully written and animated film tells the story of a young girl from a small, quiet community, who is forced to fight for her people's way of life when invaded by a much more powerful nation which attempts to use a weapon of legendary power, whose destructive force cannot be controlled.

In many major cities, specialist sf and comic shops are beginning to import tapes by other US dubbing and subtitling houses, such as LA Hero (English language producers of the new *Macross II: Lovers Again* series), Carl Macek's Streamline Pictures and US Manga Corps, who work closely with UK company Manga Entertainment Limited. These tapes aren't cheap, being priced at the same level as their US specialist market counterparts, currently around £22, and you need an NTSC video recorder and TV to watch them, but they are still selling. It appears that anime is about to become an overnight success.

Like all overnight successes, however, anime has been around in Britain for much longer than you might realise. In the late sixties and early seventies, British TV showed some American versions of popular anime shows, such as *Marine Boy* and *Battle of the Planets*, continuing in the eighties with such series as *Thunderbirds 2086*, a revamping of Gerry Anderson's concept of a future rescue team (released in Japan as *Technovoyager*), and Nagai Go's puppet series *X-Bomber*, shown on British TV as *Starfleet*. A selection of seventies robot series from Toei Doga was also available here in the late eighties on video — though not seen on TV — in an edited version from US television, as Jim Terry Production's *Force Five* (also available

in the UK on video as *Krypton Force*). The editing to fit US networks' time requirements completely destroyed the continuity of the stories and character development, but couldn't take away the novelty, excitement and curious dignity of the giant robots themselves.

Not all the translated versions of anime seen in Britain have come via the USA. European-Japanese co-productions and translations have sometimes made it to our TV screens. *Ulysses 31*, a collaboration between Japan's Tokyo Movie Shinsha (a studio with a long history of successful co-production work) and French television, was screened by the BBC. This is distinguished as both an enjoyable action adventure, retelling the story of the ancient Greek classic *The Odyssey* in futuristic settings, and as the TV singing début of then children's TV presenter Philip Schofield, now a musical star, heard on one occasion warbling the theme tune over the end credits and music! Also on BBC, viewers were able to enjoy *The Mysterious Cities of Gold*, a Japanese-French co-production from the same source, relating the adventures of orphan Esteban searching for Inca gold in the New World of the sixteenth century. Most recently, in 1991, *Samurai Pizza Cats*, known in Japan as *Kyatto Ninden Teyande*, became cult viewing for many fans far older than the usual Saturday morning TV audience. On the feature film front, the BBC have bought *Akira* for screening sometime in 1993, and Miyazaki's film *Laputa* had been shown in several regions by late 1992.

As home VCRs became more common in the mid-eighties, a number of video companies, mainly at the cheaper end of the children's market, released some anime. Most of these labels have sunk without trace and their distribution was never predictable, with the exception of Boots' own-label, Kids Cartoon Coll-ection, which put tapes like *World of the Talisman* on the shelves in every High Street for six to eight year-olds to buy.

Unfortunately, this was a somewhat self-defeating exercise. *World of the Talisman* was a redub of the complex and baffling *OAV Birth*, never intended for such young children, and sits rather oddly alongside other tapes in the collec-tion, like Tokyo Movie Shinsha's animal allegories. Much of the anime which has appeared in the UK has been packaged on children's labels because, until IWC founded Manga Video, no British company believed there was a market for 'cartoons' outside this age group. Since it was not initially intended for small children, the little success anime has enjoyed is almost miraculous.

MY-TV, a label set up in the mid-eighties specifically to release retail video for the under-sevens, included in its sadly shortlived history such goodies as *Crushers* (*Crusher Joe*, action-adventure for a teenage audience from *Dirty Pair* creator Takachiho) and *Once Upon a Time* (*Windaria*, an anti-war epic featuring extra-marital sex, treason and betrayal) — beautiful animation, but hardly ideal children's programming. The huge conglomerate Parkfield, which collapsed in 1991, produced its own kiddies label, Parkfield Playtime, featuring a similar mix of programming originally made for children and that intended for a teenage or young adult audience.

Sold into the wrong market, anime's chances of success were very limited until the launch of the Manga Video label, when the picture began to change. As the market expands, British fans can expect a wider range to be more readily available.

Previous page. Akira: *Kaneda*.
(© 1987 Akira Committee)

 Bubblegum Crash: *Priss*.

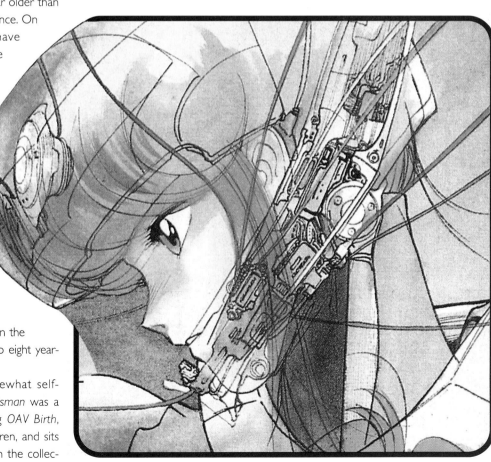

nine

the anime toyshop

Anime merchandise is a major industry in Japan, and its popularity isn't confined to its native land. For two decades or more, televised anime in Italy and France has led to a demand for anime goods there, which has been met by local companies under license from the original producers. In the USA too, merchandise has been and is being pro-. duced. In the UK, cheap Hong Kong, Taiwanese and Chinese ripoff versions of many items have crept onto the cheaper end of the toy market, and during the Transformers boom in the seventies a number of authentic Japanese items made their way here to feed the robot mania prevalent among schoolboys at that time. A constant watch on market stalls and cheap toyshops still produces the occasional Japanese item, though how and why these few oddments reach Britain is still something of a mystery. A few British companies do bring over Japanese toys for the mass market, but these have almost invariably been renamed, recoloured or in some other way adapted on the grounds that British children 'can't relate to Japanese names and ideas'. (Try that one on Sega or Nintendo.)

Dolls like these are produced for ⬇ *European as well as Japanese children.*

A few of the anime goodies readily ➡ *available in Japanese shops.*

When Japanese originals can be found, they often command high prices and are eagerly sought after by collectors a good deal older than their original target audience. The quality of design and manufacture of modern Japanese toys has begun to attract many Western enthusiasts. Specialist shops bring in some examples, particularly of model kits, which are the easiest type of Japanese merchandise to find in Britain. (A listing of a few such shops can be found in appendix one.)

MODEL KITS

Remember those ten *Gundam* kits for every inhabitant of Japan? Well, *Gundam* is the most successful series in terms of number of kits produced, but it's only one among many. Every popular series has its kit line, with not just the machines but also the characters figuring in the range. Popular charas and mecha appear as garage kits, but unpopularity is no bar — if only a few fans like a particular show, but the design is interesting and challenging, garage kit makers will often produce kits for shows overlooked by the larger companies. Some garage kit companies, like Wave, have progressed from tiny, unlicensed outfits marketing via word of mouth and fanzine ads, to large concerns producing a wide range of product under license from the rights' holders.

TOYS AND GAMES

Robots (including Transformers), vehicles, dolls, board games, cuddly soft toys — the range is huge. Again, any popular show will inspire a wide selection of toys, in precisely the same way as a successful British or American TV show is merchandised. Among the prized items in my own collection are two *Dirty Pair* dolls by Bandai, made in soft vinyl in -chan style, with moulded hair and removable costumes. These turn up for sale in collectors' magazines and a few UK suppliers have occasionally had some for sale. A good example of a

toy produced under license overseas for foreign markets is my Arale doll, made specifically for the Italian market though identical to the Japanese version.

Cute or serious, there's a kit for every major character and mecha.

Kei and Yuri in soft vinyl — Bandai's Dirty Pair dolls.

CD selection — vocal collections, image albums and symphonic fantasies as well as the usual straight soundtracks.

PAPER GOODS AND TEXTILES

A huge range of stationery items, from files and folders for schoolwork to calendars and posters, means that Japanese fans can be surrounded by their favourite characters everywhere. Collector cards, sticker albums and rubber stamps are all widely available. Especially popular, and not usually seen in the West, are CD or CD-single calendars, a number of cards packed in a CD-style jewel box and rearranged each month so that the current month's picture is on top and visible through the casing. Handkerchiefs and wall hangings are also very popular, but T-shirts prove less so. It seems the Japanese will occasionally buy T-shirts of favourite shows, but are less likely to actually wear them than Western fans. Given the Japanese view of otaku as undesirable people, perhaps it's not altogether surprising that fans are reluctant to advertise themselves in this way!

SWEETS

Rare in the West, but everyday purchases in Japan, small boxes of sweets with a tiny toy or kit sell for 100 to 250 yen and are bought by school-children. These are absolutely charming, and are beginning to be collected by anime fans in Britain, though their scarcity outside Japan makes them a real collector's challenge, and when they appear in specialist shops are usually at least between 200 and 500% more expensive than in Japan. An article on these items in *Anime UK Magazine 1*, December 1991, is, so far as I am aware, the only published information in the West.

PHONECARDS

Japan has had telephone cards since 1979 and anime phonecards are eagerly collected there, though few phonecard collectors here have as yet picked up on the craze. There is a huge range of subjects and charas portrayed on anime phonecards. Some cards are given away with magazines or manga, but many can be bought from normal phonecard outlets in Japan. An article in *Anime UK Magazine 6*, February 1993, gives advice and addresses for further information.

CDS AND LDS

Every anime production has at least a couple of CDs on the market — a soundtrack album and the theme song/s. Many have far more; for example, *The Secret of Blue Water* (the title *Fushigi No Umi No Nadia* translates as *Nadia of the Sea of Mystery*) had an eleven CD boxed set released in 1992, collecting together all the CDs based on the series and film so far released.

Laserdiscs (LD) are actually cheaper in Japan than videotapes, which are far more expensive than in the UK, so many fans buy their anime on LD. Older, classic shows, made before the advent of LD technology, are now being re-released as boxed LD sets. Imports of Japanese LDs and CDs are rare, often highly priced and hard to come by. A few reliable sources are suggested in appendix one.

The increasing popularity of anime in Britain may lead to a greater quantity of imports and easier availability of merchandise. Let's hope so!

Phonecards — hugely popular in Japan, anime cards make a change from the usual views of Fuji and corporate logos.

we want information

how to find anime shops, clubs and publications

This book has given you a short overview of the world of anime. Now you're probably wondering where to get more information. What about the thousands of shows and charas not mentioned here? How can you find out more and meet other fans? Where can you buy videos, CDs, toys and kits? This appendix will help you get started. I hope that, like me, your enjoyment of anime increases as you get to know more about the range and scope of this wonderful mixture of art form and pop culture. Good luck or, as the Japanese would say, ganbatte kudasai!

Unfortunately, not all the information published on anime is available in the UK, and it isn't all in English — or even in Japanese. French and Italian publications provide much useful information and if you read either language then the books and magazines in the bibliography are well worth your attention. For an English-speaking fan, however, this book, and the few items listed in the bibliography, are all that's generally available. The way to get more information is by writing to companies releasing anime or tapping into the international network of anime clubs. Here are a few addresses to get you started.

CLUBS AND COMPANIES

Animaster, The Goodwill Network, attention of Massimo Iorillo, PO Box 3244, 1400 Yverdon, Switzerland. Directory of anime clubs and shops worldwide and various other English language or trilingual publications. Send sae and two International Reply Coupons (from the Post Office, exchangeable for local stamps overseas) for details.

Anime Hasshin, c/o Lorraine Savage, PO Box 391036, Cambridge, MA 02139-1036, USA. Long established US club, newsletter, information packets, welcomes overseas members. Send sae and two IRCs for details.

Anime KYO, 4 St Peter's Street, Syston, Leicester LE7 8HJ. Independent fan-run club covering all

anime (not just UK releases), newsletter, information service. Send ssae for details of current membership cost.

Anime Projects, 64 Stanley Mead, Bradley Stoke, Bristol BS12 0EG. Releases AnimEigo subtitled tapes on PAL. Send ssae for details.

Japanese Animations Fans of Western Australia, c/o Tom Edge, 38 Dilkora Way, City Beach, Perth 6015, Western Australia. Newsletter, information, British fans especially welcome; send sae and three IRCs for details.

The Manga Club, 40 St Peter's Road, London W6 9BD. Send ssae for information on Manga Video releases. Membership free, newsletter, promotional goodies

Manga Entertainment Limited, address as for The Manga Club. Releases dubbed anime on PAL.

Summer Side, c/o Alec Orrock, 24161-H Hollyoak, Laguna Hills, CA 92656, USA. Newsletter, information service, overseas members welcome. Send sae and two IRCs for details.

Western Connection, Suite 18, 37 Westbourne Terrace, London W2. Released *The Sensualist*, other anime plans unknown. Send ssae for information.

The international computer network INTERNET

offers worldwide access to anime bulletin boards, conferences and databases. Many colleges, polytechnics and universities in Britain can access the network direct. INTERNET addresses can change, so the best way to get current details is via an anime club or directory.

TOYS AND OTHER GOODIES

Shops in the UK selling anime goods are few and far between, and even in the USA there aren't many retail outlets offering a wide range of goods. There's also the problem that in any economic climate shops may close down, or change hands and stock policy, or cease to offer a mail order service. Write to or telephone the shop (not forgetting the usual ssae for British enquiries and sae plus two to three IRCs for overseas) before you send any money or visit, especially if it involves a long journey. World video and TV standards vary, so when buying a video cassette recorder, laserdisc player or any tapes or discs, make sure you know that they are compatible with your existing equipment.

Try the following addresses for videos, LDs and anime goods.

Animaster (address under clubs section) sells anime laserdiscs and CDs by mail order at reasonable prices. Send two IRCs for details.

Books Nippon, 64-66 St Paul's Churchyard, London EC4M 8AA, tel 071 248 4956. Shop serving the London Japanese community. Books, magazines, gifts and an excellent mail order service which can get you any book or magazine currently in print in Japan.

Cannon and Co, 18 Newport Place, London WC2, tel 071 437 7157. Chinese book, gift and video shop sells anime magazines from Hong Kong and anime videos on PAL (British standard) dubbed into Chinese. Mail order service.

Comet Miniatures, 44-46 Lavender Hill, Battersea, London SW11, tel 071 228 3702. Model kits, including imports direct from Japan. Mail order service.

Forbidden Planet, 71 New Oxford Street, London WC1, tel 071 836 4179. Science fiction/telefantasy and comics plus anime magazines, translated manga, badges, t-shirts, model kits and videos. Mail order service.

Hobby Bounties, 865 Mountbatten Road, #02-77, Katong Shopping Centre, Singapore 1543, tel 0101 65 440 1890. Model kits from Japan, good prices. Mail order service.

Hunter SRL, Via Calvart 34, 40129 Bologna, Italy. Anime videos, manga, stationery and posters. Mail order service.

Japan Centre, 212 Piccadilly, London W1V 9LD, tel 071 439 8035. Another shop serving the London Japanese community, with books, magazines, manga, language study aids and a sushi bar.

Japanimation Delivery Service, 11 rue des Chapeliers, 3000 Nimes, France, tel 010 33 66 67 84 67. LDs, CDs, models, manga and video on PAL and SECAM; 'all product made in Japan'. Mail order service.

Laser Perceptions, 1739 Noriega Street, San Francisco, CA 94122, USA, tel 0101 415 752 2016. Anime laserdiscs and CDs. Mail order service.

Librairie Tonkam, 29 rue Keller, 75011 Paris, France, tel 010 33 1 47 00 78 38. Manga, magazines, books, posters, laserdiscs, CDs, cells and more. Mail order service.

Metropolis, 6 rue du Palais de Justice, 69005 Lyon, France, tel 010 33 72 41 92 58. Manga, magazines, books, CDs, LDs, posters, model kits, cells, etc. Mail order service.

Nikaku Animart, 615 N 6th Street, San Jose, CA 95112, USA, tel 0101 408 971 2822. Japanese gift shop, also selling one of the best ranges of anime goods anywhere outside Japan, with a mail order service it is impossible to praise too highly. Two IRCs brings information on their latest anime list packed with toys, stationery, CDs,

posters and books. Simply the best service I've ever found.

OCS Books, Grosvenor Parade, Uxbridge Road, London W5, tel 081 992 6335. Japanese magazines, books and manga.

The Sheffield Space Centre, 33 The Wicker, Sheffield S3 8HS, tel 0742 758905. Wide anime stock of books, posters, cells, kits and magazines, friendly and informed staff. Mail order service.

Top Ten Soho, Unit 3, 9-12 St Anne's Court, London W1V 3AX, tel 071 734 7388. Manga, books, kits and videos. Ordering service for US goods.

BIBLIOGRAPHY

All publications are in English unless otherwise stated. Contact the publishers or ask at your local specialist sf or comic shop for ordering details and current availability.

MAGAZINES

Animag, irregular US magazine published by Eclipse, PO Box 31492, San Francisco, CA 91361, USA.

Animeland, quarterly French language magazine published by Animarte, 15 rue de Phalsbourg, 75017 Paris, France.

Animerica, monthly US magazine, also includes translated manga, published by Viz Communications Inc, 440 Brannan Street, San Francisco, CA 94107, USA. Viz also publishes a wide range of translated manga.

Anime UK Magazine, bimonthly British magazine published by Anime UK Ltd, 70 Mortimer Street, London W1.

Kappa Magazine, monthly Italian language magazine, colour features and b/w manga in Italian, published by Edizioni Star Comics srl, Via di Vallingegno 2/a, Bosco, PG Italy.

Manga Mania, monthly b/w magazine, manga strips and articles, published by Dark Horse International, 16-24 Underwood Street, London N1 9EF.

Mangazine, monthly Italian language magazine, colour features and b/w manga in Italian, published by Granata Press, via Marconi no 47, 40122 Bologna, Italy.

Mecha Press, bimonthly Canadian anime game/kit magazine, published by Ianvs Publications, 2360 Ave de LaSalle, #211, Montreal, Quebec, Canada H1V 2L1.

Protoculture Addicts, bimonthly Canadian magazine published by Ianvs Publications, address as for *Mecha Press*.

Super Play, monthly dedicated Super Nintendo Entertainment System magazine carries regular anime and manga columns, published by Future Publishing, Cary Court, Somerton, Somerset, TA11 6TB.

Tsunami, bimonthly French language magazine published by Durendal, 1 rue Eugene Varlin, 93170 Bagnolet, France.

BOOKS

Cartoonia Anime, Guida al Cinema di Animazione Giapponese, by Baricordi, de Giovanni, Pietroni, Rossi and Tunesi, Italian language, published by Granata Press (address as for *Mangazine*), 1991, ISBN 88-7248-14-0.

Manga, catalogue for the exhibition Manga, Comic Strip Books from Japan, at the Pomeroy Purdey Gallery, London, Oct-Nov 1991; includes strips by Tezuka and others, essays by Paul Gravett and Helen McCarthy, published by Lowe Culture, 1991, ISBN 1-873184-02-6.

Manga Manga Manga A Celebration of Japanese animation at the ICA Cinema, by Helen McCarthy, published by Island World Communications, 1992, ISBN 0-9520434-0-8, to coincide with the season of anime shown at the ICA.

Manga! Manga! The World of Japanese Comics, by Frederick L. Schodt, published by Kodansha International, 1983.

Il Mondo dei Manga, by Thierry Groensteen, Italian language translated from the French by Carlotti and Fornaroli, excellent bibliography for further reading, published by Granata Press, 1991, ISBN 88-7248-013-2.

ARTICLES

Anime Rising by Jeff Yang, *Village Voice*, November 1992.

A to Z of Anime by Steve Kyte, *Anime UK Magazine*, Dec 1991-ongoing.

Heavy Metal Heaven — A History of the Robot in Anime by Steve Kyte, privately printed for circulation at the 1990 National Science Fiction Convention, reprinted by author's permission 1992 *Anime Kyo News*.

index of featured anime productions

Each production is indexed by the English language title most often used, or if no commonly used form exists, by the original Japanese title, written in romaji (English script). Just to confuse things, the original Japanese title may be in English — many foreign words are used in this way. Where no Japanese title is given, it is identical with the English version. The information is presented as follows: Japanese titles in romaji, and any other important variant titles are given for each entry; the type of production (ie whether film, TV series or OAV), along with number of episodes or running time where known; the director (dir); the copyright holder; UK releases or TV screenings where known; and finally, information on spin-off series, films, etc.

A

Aim for the Ace! (1973): Jap *Ace O Nerae*; Italy *Jenny la Tennista*; Italy/France *Jenny Jenny*. TV series, 26 episodes. Dir: Dezaki Osamu. Yamamoto S/TMS.
also: (1) Film, 85 min. Yamamoto S/TMS.
(2) *Ace O Nerae II* (1988). OAV series, 6 episodes. Yamamoto S/TMS.

Akira (1987): Film, 124 min. Dir: Otomo Katsuhiro. Akira Committee. UK release 1991 on Island World Communications.

Anpan Man (1991): TV series, 30 min. NTV.

Astro Boy (1963): Jap *Tetsuwan Atom*; Eng *Iron-Arm Atom*. TV series, 193 episodes. Mushi.

Aura Battler Dunbine (1983): Jap *Seisenshi Dunbine*. TV series, 49 episodes. Nippon Sunrise.
also: (1) OAV series, 3 episodes. 1988. Nippon Sunrise.

B

Bats & Terry (1987): Film, 80 min. Nippon Sunrise.

Battle of the Planets: see under *Gatchaman*.

Black Magic M(ario): 66 (1987): OAV, 48 min. Shirow M/Animate Film.

Bubblegum Crisis (1987-): OAV series. AIC/Artmic/Network. UK release commencing 1992 on Anime Projects label (eight tapes).

C

Cagliostro Castle: see under *Lupin III*.

Captain Harlock (1978): *Uchu Kaizoku Captain Harlock*; Eng *Space Pirate Captain Harlock*. TV series, 42 episodes. Matsumoto R/TV Asahi/Toei Doga.
also: (1) Film, 1978. Subtitled *Arcadia Go No Nazo*;

Eng *The Mystery of Arcadian*. 151 min. As above.
(2) Film, 1982. Subtitled *Waga Seishun No Arcadia*; Eng *My Youth in Arcadia*. 130 min. Matsumoto R/Tokyu Agency/Toei.
(3) TV series, 1982. Subtitled as above, plus *Mugen Kido SSX*; Eng *Endless Road SSX*. 22 episodes. As above.

Cat's Eye (1983/4): TV series, 73 episodes. Dir: (part 1, 36 episodes) Takeuchi Yoshio, (part 2, 37 episodes) Kodama Kenji. Hojo T/Shueisha/TMS.

CB Go Nagai World (1991): OAV. Dynamic Planning Co.

Champion, The (1970): Jap *Ashita No Joe*; Italy *Rocky Joe*. TV series, 79 episodes. Dir: Takamori A/Chiba T. Chiba T/Takamori A/Mushi Prod.
also: (1) Film (1981), 110 min. Dir: Dezaki Osamu. Takamori A/Tetsuya C/TMS.

Char's Counterattack (1988): Jap *Kido Senshi v Gundam: Gyakushu No Char*. Film, 120 min. Nippon Sunrise.

Chibi Maruko-Chan (1990): TV series. SM/C/NA.

Chikara To Onna No Yononaka (1932): Eng *The World of Power and Women*. Film. Dir: Masaoka Kenzo.

City Hunter (1987): TV series, 52 episodes. Hojo T/Shueisha/Sunrise.
also: (1) TV series (1988), 62 episodes. Hojo T/Shueisha/Sunrise.
(2) TV series (1989), 12 episodes. As above.
(3) *City Hunter 91* (1991). TV series, 13 episodes. As above.
(4) *A Magnum of Love's Destiny* (1988). Film. As above.
(5) *Bay City Wars* (1990). OAV.
(6) *The Million Dollar Conspiracy* (1990). OAV.

Cobra (1982): Jap *Space Cobra*. TV series, 31 episodes. Dir: Dezaki O/Takeuchi Y. Terasawa Buichi/TMS.

also: (1) *Space Adventure Cobra* (1982). Film, 99 min. Terasawa Buichi/TMS.

Cream Lemon (1984-): longrunning erotic OAV series. Soeishinsha.

Crushers (1983): Jap *Crusher Joe*. Film, 125 min. Nippon Sunrise. UK release 1988 on MY-TV label.

Cyber City Oedo 808 (1990): OAV series, 3 episodes. Japan Home Video.

Dallos (1983): Jap *Dallos Hakai Shirei*; Eng *Dallos Power of Destruction*. OAV (first of series). Studio Pierrot/Network.

Danguard Ace (1977): Jap *Planet Robot Danguard Ace*. TV series, 56 episodes. Toei. UK video release as part of edited *Force Five* series on Video Brokers label and re-release as *Krypton Force* on unnamed label.

Devilman (1972): TV series, 39 episodes. Nagai Go/Dynamic Prod.
also: (1) *Devilman Tanjo Hen* (*Devilman: The Origin*) (1987). OAV, 51 min. Nagai Go/Dynamic Planning/Triangle/Kodansha.
(2) *Devilman II* (1990). OAV, 50 min. Nagai Go/Dynamic Planning/Bandai.

Dino Mech Gaiking: see under *Gaiking*.

Dirty Pair (1985): Italy *Kate & July*; France *Dan et Dany*. TV series, 24 episodes. Takachiho and Studio Nue/Sunrise/NTV.
also: (1) *The Nolandia Affair* (1985). OAV, 55 min. Subtitled *Nolandia No Nazo*. As above.
(2) *Dirty Pair* (1987). Eng *Project Eden*. Film, 80 min. As above.
(3) *Dirty Pair: From Lovely Angels With Love* (1988). OAV, 47 min. *Dirty Pair: Lovely Angels Yori Ai O Komete*. Takachiho/Sunrise/VAP Video
(4) OAV series, 9 episodes. VAP Video. Takachiho/Sunrise.
(5) *Flight 005 Conspiracy* (1990). OAV. As above.

Dr Slump & Aralechan (1981): TV series, 243 episodes. Dir: Okazaki Minoru. Bird Studio/Shueisha/Fuji TV/Toei Doga.
also: (1) Film (1981). Subtitled *Hello! Wonderland*. 25 min. As above.
(2) Film (1983). Subtitled *Hoyoyo! Sekai Isshu Dai Race* (*The Great Round-the-world Race*). 75 min. As above.
(3) Film (1984). Subtitled *Hoyoyo! Nanabajo No Hiho* (*The Secret Treasure of Nanaba Castle*). 48 min. As above.
(4) Film (1985). Subtitled *Hoyoyo! Yume No Miyako Mechapolis* (*The Capital of Dreams*). 38 min. As above.

Dominion (1988): OAV series, 4 episodes. Agent 21/Toshiba Eizo Soft. UK release 1992 on Manga Video (2 tapes).

Doraemon (1973): TV series, 27 episodes. Fujiko Fujio/Nihon TV Doga.
also: (1) TV series (1979-). Fujiko Fujio/Shin'ei Doga.
Plus too many films to list in this space!

Eight Man (1963): Eng *8th Man*. TV series, 56 episodes. TCJ.

Fire Tripper (1985): Jap *Rumic World — Hono Tripper*. OAV, 48 min. Takahashi R/ Shogakkan/Kitty/Fuji TV. Part of *Rumic World* series of unconnected OAVs.

Fist of the North Star (1984): Jap *Hokuto No Ken*; Eng *Ken of the Great Bear School*. TV series, 109 episodes. Hara T/Buronson/Shueisha/Toei Doga.
also: (1) TV series (1987), 43 episodes. As above.
(2) Film (1986). As above. UK release 1992 on Manga Video.

Force Five (1980/81): US syndicated TV series, 130 episodes. Jim Terry Production. Made up of 26 edited episodes each of the following series: (1) *UFO Robot Grendizer*, Eng *Grandizer*; (2) *Danguard Ace*; (3) *Dino Mech Gaiking*, Eng *Gaiking*; (4) *Starzinger*, Eng *Spaceketeers*; (5) *Getta Robot G*, Eng *Starvengers*. UK video release on Video Brokers label and re-release as *Krypton Force* on unnamed label.

Gaiking (1976): Jap *Dino Mech Gaiking*; Eng *Space Dragon Gaiking*. TV series, 44 episodes. Toei. UK video release as part of edited *Force Five* series on Video Brokers Label and re-release as *Krypton Force* on unnamed label.

Gall Force (1986): Subtitled *Eternal Story*. OAV, 86 min. Artmic/AIC.
also: (1) OAV (1987). Subtitled *Destruction*. 50 min. Animate/Artmic/AIC.
(2) OAV (1988). Subtitled *Stardust War*. 60 min. Artmic/AIC/Sony.
(3) *The Ten Little Gall Force* (1988). SD parody OAV, 30 min. Artmic/Sony.

Gatchaman (1972): Jap *Kagaku Ninjatai Gatchaman*; Eng trans *Science Ninja Team Gatchaman*. TV series, 105 episodes. Tatsunoko.
also: (1) Film (1978). 110 min. Tatsunoko.
(2) *Kagaku Ninjatai Gatchaman II* (1978). TV series, 52 episodes. Tatsunoko (both series edited for USA as *Battle of the Planets* and *G-Force*).

(3) *Kagaku Ninjatai Gatchaman F* (1979). Eng *Gatchaman Fighter*. TV series, 48 episodes. Tatsunoko. Some UK releases on various now defunct labels in 1980; also shown on UK TV.

Genesis Survivor Gaiarth (1991): OAV series, 2 episodes. 50 min. Toshiba EMI.

Georgie (1983): Jap *Lady Georgie*. TV series, 40 episodes. Dir: Yoshida Shigetsugu. Igarashi Y/Izawa M/TMS.

Getta Robot G: see under *Starvengers*.

G-Force: see under *Gatchaman*.

Gigantor (1963): Jap *Tetsujin 28-GO*; Eng *Iron Man No. 28*. TV series, 96 episodes. TCJ.
also: (1) TV series (1980). 51 episodes. Dir: Imazawa Tetsuo. Hikari Prod/TMS.
(2) *Tetsujin 28-GO FX* (1992). TV series, 41 episodes. Dir: Kamegaki Hajime. Hikari Prod/TMS/NAS/NTV.

God Mars (1981): Jap *Rokushin Gattai God Mars*; Eng *God Mars — Six Gods United in One Body*. TV series, 64 episodes. Dir: Imazama Tetsuo. Hikaru Prod/TMS.
also: (1) Film (1982). 100 min. As above.
(2) OAV (1988). Subtitled *Junanasai No Densetsu*; Eng *17-year-old's Legend*. 56 min. As above.

God Mazinger (1984): Eng *The Deity*. TV series, 23 episodes. Dir: Okuwaki Masaharu, Kodama Kenji. Nagai Go/Dynamic Planning/TMS.

Golgo 13 (1983): Eng *The Professional*. Film, 95 min. Dir: Dezaki Osamu. Saitoh Takao/Saitoh Prod/TMS.

Grandizer (1975): Jap *UFO Robot Grendizer*; France/Italy *Goldorak*. TV series, 74 episodes. Dynamic Prod/TV Asahi/Toei Doga.
also: (1) *UFO Robot Grendizer Tai Great Mazinger* (1976). Eng *UFO Robot Grenzider Against Great Mazinger*. Film, 27 min. As above.
(2) *Grenzider, Getta Robot G. Great Mazinger — Kessen Daikaiju* (1976). Eng *Grandizer, Getta Robot G Great Mazinger — Battle Against the Great Sea Monster*. Film, 31 min. As above. UK video release as part of the heavily edited *Force Five* series on Video Brokers label, also as part of *Krypton Force* on unnamed label.

Great Mazinger (1974): TV series, 56 episodes. Dir: Katsumata T/Tamiya T/Akehi M/Sankichi Y/Imazawa D/Onuki N. Nagai Go/Dynamic Planning/Toei Doga.

Gundam: see under *Mobile Suit Gundam* and *SD Gundam*.

H

Hakujaden (1958): Eng *The White Serpent*. 78 min. Dir. Yabushita Taiji. Toei Doga.

Hell City Shinjuku (1988): Jap *Magai Toshi Shinjuku*. OAV, 80 min. Madhouse/Japan Home Video.

Hello Spank! (1981): Jap *Ohayo Spank!*. TV series, 63 episodes. Dir. Yoshida Shigetsugu. Takanashi Shizue/Yukimuro Shunichi/TMS.
also: (1) Film (1982). 90 min. Dir. Yoshida Shigetsugo. Yukimuro Shunichi/Takanashi Shizue/TMS.

I

Iron Man no 28: see under *Gigantor*.

J

Joker Marginal City (1992): OAV, 30 min. Michihara K.

K

Kiki's Delivery Service (1989): Jap *Majo No Takkyubin*; Eng *Witch's Express Delivery*. Film, 105 min. Dir. Miyazaki Hayao. Nibariki/Tokuma Shoten.

Kitaro Gegege (1968): Jap *Ge Ge Ge No Kitaro*. TV series, 65 episodes. Toei Doga/Fugi TV.
also: (1) TV series (1985). 108 episodes. Toei Doga/Fuji TV.
(2) Film (1985). 39 min. Mizuwi Prod/Toei Doga.
(3) Film (1986). Subtitled *Yokai Diasenso*; Eng *The Great Ghost War*. 39 min. Mizuki S/Toei Doga.
(4) Film (1986). Subtitled *Saikyo Yokai Gundan! Nihonjoriku*; Eng *Devastating Monsters Arrive in Japan*. 49 min. Mizuki S/Toei Doga.
(5) Film (1986). Subtitled *Gekitotsu! Ijigen Yokai No Dai Hanran*; Eng *The Great Revolt of Monsters from Another Dimension*. 49 min. Mizuki S/Toei Doga.

L

Laputa (1986): Jap *Tenku No Shiro Rapyuta*; Eng *Laputa: Castle in the Sky*. Film, 195 min. Dir. Miyazaki Hayao. Nibariki/Tokuma Shoten. Shown on UK TV.

Laughing Target, The (1987): Jap *Rumic World — Warau Hyoteki*. OAV, 509 min. Takahashi R/Shogakkan/Kitty/Pony. Part of *Rumic World* series of unconnected OAVs.

Legend of Galactic Heroes (1988): Jap *Ginga Heiya Densetsu*. Film. Subtitled *Across the Sea of Stars* (*Wagayuku Wa Hoshi No Umi*).
also: (1) OAV (1988). 26 episodes. Tanaka Y/Tokuma Shoten/Kitty Film.

(2) OAV (1992). 26 episodes. As above.

Legend of the Demon Womb: see under *Urotsukidoji: Legend of the Overfiend*.

Legend of the Overfiend: see under *Urotsukidoji: Legend of the Overfiend*.

Lensman (1984): Jap *SF Shinseiki — Lensman*; Eng *SF New Century - Lensman*. Film, 108 min. Dir. Hirokawa/Kawajiri. E.E. 'Doc' Smith/Kodansha. UK release 1993 on Manga Video label.

Lupin III (1971/1977/1984): Jap *Lupin Sansei*; Eng *Cliff Hanger*. Three TV series, 228 episodes in total. Dir. (part 1, 23 episodes) Okuma M/Takahata I/Miyazaki H, (part 2, 155 episodes) Mikuriya K/Mikamoto Y/Yoshida S, (part 3, 50 episodes) Aoki Y. Monkey Punch/NTV/YTV/TMS.

Other *Lupin III* productions:
Cagliostro Castle (1979): Jap *Lupin Sansei — Cagliostro No Shiro*. Film, 100 min. Dir. Miyazaki Hayao. Monkey Punch/TMS.

Secret of Mamo (1978): Jap *Lupin Sansei — Mamo Karano Chousen*. Film, 100 min. Dir. Yoshikawa Soji. Monkey Punch/TMS.

Gold of Babylon (1985): Jap *Lupin Sansei — Babilon No Ogon Densetsu*. Film, 100 min. Monkey Punch/Toho.

Plot of the Fuma Clan (1987): Jap *Lupin Sansei — Fuma No Ichizoku No Inbo*. Film, 75 min. Monkey Punch/Toho.

Bye Bye Liberty (1989): Film, 120 min. Monkey Punch.

M

Macross (1982): Jap *Chojiku Yosai Macross*; Eng *Super Dimensional Fortress Macross*. TV series, 36 episodes. Big West.
also: (1) *Do You Remember Love?* (1984). Film, 112 min. *Ai Oboetaimasuka*. Big West.

Macross II: Lovers Again (1992): OAV, 6 episodes. Dir. Yatagai Kenichi. Big West/Macross II Project.

Magical Princess Minky Momo (1982): Jap *Maho No Princess Minky Momo*. TV series, 63 episodes. Ashi.
also: (1) Film (1985). Subtitled *La Ronde in My Dream*. 80 min. Ashi.

Maison Ikkoku (1986): TV series, 96 episodes. Takahashi R/Shogakkan/Kitty/Fuji TV.

Manga Calendar (1962): TV series, 54 episodes. Otagi.

Marine Boy (1969): Jap *Kaitei Shonen Marin*. TV series, 13 episodes. TV Doga. Shown on UK TV.

Mazinger Z (1972): TV series, 92 episodes. Dir. Serikawa Y/Katsumata T/Onuki N/Nagaki B. Dynamic Prod/Toei Doga. UK video release on now defunct Mountain Video label.

Metal Skin Panic Madox — 01 (1987): OAV, 50 min. AIC. UK release 1993 on Anime Projects label.

Mobile Suit Gundam (1979): Jap *Kido Senshi Gundam*. TV series, 43 episodes. Sotsu Agency/Nippon Sunrise. Edited into three feature films; *Mobile Suit Gundam I*, *MS Gundam II — Love Warrior* (Jap *Ai Senshi*), and *MS Gundam III — Lovers Meet in Space* (Jap *Meguriai Sorahen*).

Other *Gundam* productions:
MS Zeta Gundam (1985): Jap *Kido Senshi Z Gundam*. TV series, 50 episodes. Sotsu Agency/Sunrise.

MS Gundam F91 (1991): Jap *Kido Senshi Gundam F91*. Film. As above.

MS Gundam: Remnants of Zion (1992): Jap *Zion No Zenko*. Film. As above.

MS Gundam 0080 — A War in the Pocket/ MS Gundam 0083 — Stardust Memory (1990/ 1992): OAV, 8 episodes/13 episodes. As above.

V-Gundam (1993-): TV series. Sunrise. No other information currently available.

Momotaro (1918): Film. Dir. Kitayama Seitaro.

Mon Pe (1982): Jap *Tonde Monpe*. TV series, 42 episodes. Dir. Yoshida Shigetsugu. ASATSU/TMS.

Mospeada (1983): Jap *Kikososeiki Mospeada*; Eng *Genesis Climber Mospeada*. TV series, 25 episodes. Tatsunoko.
also: (1) *Love Live Alive*, music video.

My Neighbour Totoro (1988): Jap *Tonari No Totoro*. Film, 85 min. Dir. Miyazaki Hayao. Nibariki/Tokuma Shoten.

My Patraasche (1992): Jap *Flanders No Inu, Boku No Patorasshu*; Eng *A Dog of Flanders*. TV series, 26 episodes. Dir. Kodama Kenji. NTV/TMS.

Mysterious Cities of Gold, The (1982): France *Les Mysterieuses Cites d'Or*. TV series, 39 episodes. Dir. Chalopin J/Deyries B/Murakami K/Maruyama K. DIC/NHK, Japanese-French co-production for French TV. Shown on UK TV.

Nausicaa of the Valley of the Wind (1983): Jap *Kaze No Tani No Nausicaa*; Eng *Warriors of the Wind*. Film, 118 min. Dir: Miyazaki Hayao. Nibariki/Tokuma Shoten/Hakuhodo/Toei. UK release on Vestron Video, re-release 1993 on First International label.

Once Upon a Time (1986): Jap *Windaria*. OAV, 101 min. Victor. UK release 1989 on MY-TV label.

Orguss (1983): Jap *Chojiku Seiki Orguss*; Eng *Super Dimensional Century Orguss*. TV series, 26 episodes. Dir: Ishiguro N/Yasuyoshi M. Big West/TMS.

Patlabor (1988): Jap *Kido Keisatsu Patlabor*; Eng *Mobile Police Patlabor*. OAV, 7 episodes. Dir: Oshii Mamoru. Tokuma Shoten/Bandai.
also: (1) Two TV series (1989/1990). As above.
(2) Film (1990). As above.

Porco Rosso (1992): Jap *Kurenai No Buta*; Eng *Crimson Pig*. Film, 120 min. Dir: Miyazaki Hayao. Nibariki/Tokuma Shoten.

Project A-KO (1986): Film, 80 min. Fairy Dust/APPP/Final Nishijima. UK release 1992 on Manga Video label.
also: (1) OAV (1987). Subtitled *Daitokuki Zaibatsu No Inbo*; Eng *Plot of Financial Group Daitokuji*. 50 min. As above.
(2) OAV (1988). Subtitled *Cinderella Rhapsody*. 50 min. As above.
(3) OAV (1989). Subtitled *The Final*. 50 min. As above.
(4) *A-KO The VS* (1990) Two part OAV series. As above.

Ranma 1/2 (1990): Jap *Ranma Nibun No Ichi*. TV series. Takahashi/Kitty Film.

Record of Lodoss War (1990): OAV, 13 episodes. Dir: Nagao Akinori. Mizuno/Group SNE/Kadokawa.

Rescue Kids, The (1991): Jap *Kinku Hasshin Seibah Kizzu*. TV series, 50 episodes. Dir: Kamegaki Hajime. Monkey Punch/Sotsu Agency/TMS.

Riding Bean (1989): OAV, 46 min. Youmex. UK release 1993 on Anime Projects label.

Robotech (1985): TV series edited from ele-ments of *Macross*, *Southern Cross* and *Mospeada* (qv). Harmony Gold. *Codename: Robotech* UK release 1989 on Kids Cartoon Collection label; shown on cable TV.
also: (1) *Robotech II: The Sentinels*. UK release 1993 on Video Gems label.

Rose of Versailles (1979): Jap *Berusaiya No Bara*; Italy/France *Lady Oscar*. TV series, 40 episodes. Dir: Nagahama Yadao, Dezaki Osamu. Ikeda Ryoko/TMS.

Samurai Pizza Cats (1990): Jap *Kyatto Ninden Teyande*. TV series, 49 episodes. Tatsunoko. Some episodes, UK release 1992 on Saban/Entertainment UK label; shown on UK TV.

Scramble Wars (1992): OAV, 30 min. Artmic.

SD Gundam (1988): Jap *Kido Senshi Super Deformed Gundam*. Film, 30 min. Bandai/Sunrise. also: further films/OAVs.

Secret of Blue Water, The (1990): Jap *Fushigi No Umi No Nadia*; Eng *Nadia of the Sea of Mystery*. TV series, 39 episodes. Dir: Anno Hideaki/Sadamoto Yoshiyuki. NHK/Sogovision/Toho. also: (1) Film (1991). As above.

Sensualist, The (1990): Film. Dir: Abe Yukio. OB Planning Co/Studio JAMP Co. UK release 1993 on Western Connection label.

Silent Moebius/Silent Moebius 2 (1991/93): Two films. Dir: Kikuchi/Tomizawa. Asamiya Kia/Studio Tron/Kadokawa Shoten/Pioneer LDC.

Southern Cross (1984): Jap *Chojiku Kishidan Southern Cross*; Eng *Super Dimensional Cavalry Southern Cross*. TV series, 23 episodes. Tatsunoko.

Space Adventure Cobra: see under *Cobra*.

Space Battleship Yamato (1974): Jap *Uchu Senkan Yamato*; Eng *Space Cruiser Yamato*, *Star Blazers*. TV series, 26 episodes. Westcape Corp.
also: (1) Film (1977). 130 min. As above.
(2) TV series II (1978). 26 episodes. As above.
(3) Film (1979). Subtitled *Aratanaru Tabidachi*; Eng *Be Forever Yamato*. 120 min. Academy Seisaki.
(4) TV series III (1980). 25 episodes. As above.
(5) Film (1983). Subtitled *Kanketsuhen*; Eng *Final Yamato*. 160 min. Westcape.
(6) *Arrivederci Yamato*. Film.

Space Cobra: see under *Cobra*.

Space Fantasia R2001 (1987): Jap *Nisen Ichi Ya Monogatari*. OAV, 60 min. Dir: Yoshida Shigetsugu. Hoshino Y/Takanashi S/TMS.

Space Firebird (1980): Jap *Hi No Tori 2772 — Ai No Cosmozone*; Eng *Phoenix 2772 — Love's Cosmozone*. Film, 121 min. Dir: Sugiyama Taki. Tezuka Prod. UK video release on now-defunct Mountain Video label.

Spacekeeters (1978): Jap *Starzinger*. TV series, 73 episodes. Toei. UK video release as part of edited *Force Five* series on Video Brokers label and re-release as *Krypton Force* on unnamed label.

Space Pirate Captain Harlock: see under *Captain Harlock*.

Starfleet (1980): Jap *X-Bomber*. TV series, puppet animation. Dynamic Planning/Fuji TV. UK release 1989 on MY-TV label.

Starvengers (1975): Jap *Getta Robot G*; Eng *Jet Robot*. TV series, 39 episodes. Dynamic Planning/Fuji TV/Toei Doga. UK video release as part of edited *Force Five* series on Video Brokers label and re-release as *Krypton Force* on unnamed label.

Starzinger: see under *Spacekeeters*.

Steel Robot Jeeg (1975): Jap *Koutetsu Jeeg*. TV series, 46 episodes. Dir: Nitta Y/Miyazaki K/Aheki M/Serikawa Y/Ochiai M. Dynamic Prod/TV Asahi/Toei Doga.

Story of a Certain Street Corner, The (1962): Jap *Aru Machikado No Monogatari*. Film, 38 min. Mushi.

Supernatural Beast City (1987): Jap *Yoju Toshi*; Eng *Monster City*. OAV. 80 min. Madhouse/JHV. 1993 UK release on Manga Video label.

Tetsujin 28: see under *Gigantor*.

Tetsuwan Atom: see under *Astro Boy*.

3 x 3 Eyes (1991): Jap *Sazan Eyes*. OAV, 4 episodes. Takada/Kodansha/Plex/Star Child. UK release 1993 on Manga Video label.

Thunderbirds 2086 (1982): Jap *Kagaku Kyujotai Technovoyager*; Eng *Technovoyager — Scientific Rescue Team*. TV series, 18 episodes. Jin. Shown on UK TV; UK video release on ITC label and others.

Touch (1985): TV series, 101 episodes. Adachi M/Shogakkan/Toho/Asatsu.
also: (1) Film (1986). Subtitled *Sebango No Nai Ace*; Eng *Ace Is No Back Number*. 93 min. As above.
(2) Film (1986). Subtitled *Sayonara No Okurimono*; Eng *Goodbye Present*. 80 min. As above.

(3) Film (1987). Subtitled *Kimi Ga Torisugita Ato Ni*. Eng *Faces of Passing Feelings*. As above.

Twins at St Clare's (1991): Jap *Ochame Na Futago*. TV series, 26 episodes. Dir: Okuwaki Masaharu. Darrel Waters Ltd/NTV/TMS.

Uchu Senkan Yamato: see under *Space Cruiser Yamato*.

Ulysses 31 (1981/1988): Jap *Uchu Densetsu Ulysses 31*; Eng *Space Legend Ulysses 31*. TV series, 31 episodes. Dir: Nagahama Tadao. TMS/DIC, Japanese-French co-production. Shown on UK TV; UK video release.

Urotsukidoji: Legend of the Overfiend (1987): Jap *Chojin Densetsu Urotsukidoji*; Eng *The Wandering Kid*; Eng trans *Legend of the Superbeing — The Wandering Kid*. OAV series. Dir: Takayama Hideki. Maeda I/Javn.
also: (1) Two feature films, *Legend of the Overfiend* (1989) and *Legend of the Demon Womb* (1989), edited from OAVs. Maeda I/Javn/Westcape. First film UK release 1992 on Manga Video label, second in 1993.

Urusei Yatsura (1981): TV series, 218 episodes.
Takahashi/Shogakkan/Kitty Film.
also: (1) *Only You* (1983). Film, 91 min. As above.
(2) *Beautiful Dreamer* (1984). Film, 98 min. As above.
(3) *Remember My Love* (1985). Film, 90 min. As above.
(4) *Lum the Forever* (1986). Film, 94 min. As above.
(5) *Lamu No Mirai Wa Donarucca* (1987). Eng *What Future for Lum?*. Film. As above.
(6) *Last Movie — Boy Meets Girl* (1988). Film, 40 min. As above.
(7) *Nagisa No Fiances* (1988). Eng *Nagisa's Fiance*. Film, 30 min. As above.
(8) *Ikari No Sharbet* (1988). Eng *Angry Sherbet*. Film, 30 min. As above.

Vampire Princess Miyu (1988): Jap *Vampire Miyu Daiichiwa Ayakashi No Miyako*; Eng *Miyu the Vampire Part 1, Ghost City*. OAV, 30 min. AIC/Soeishinsha.
also: (1) second and third OAVs (1988). 30 min. AIC/Soeishinsha. Released 1992 on AnimEigo label.

Wandering Kid: see under *Urotsukidoji*.

Warriors of the Wind: see under *Nausicaa of the Valley of the Wind*.

Windaria: see under *Once Upon a Time*.

World of the Talisman (1983): Jap *Birth*. OAV, 80 min. Victor. UK release 1989 on Kids Cartoon Collection label.

X-Bomber: see under *Starfleet*.

Genesis Survivor Gaiarth.